TANGRAM BLOCKS™ *Explorations*

Grades K–4

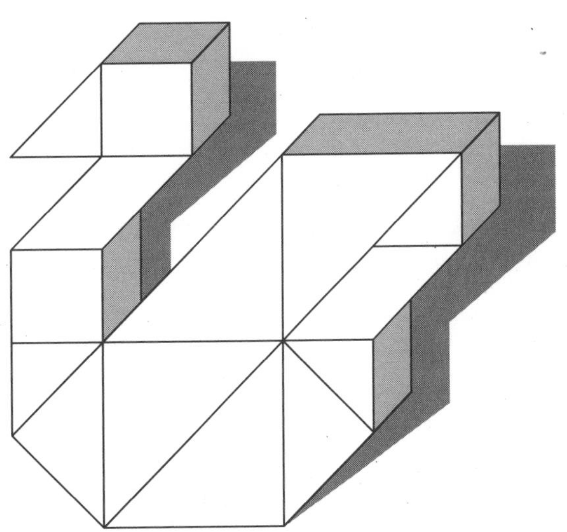

Marian Pasternack
Linda Silvey

Cuisenaire Company of America, Inc.

Acknowledgments

The authors wish to thank the following people for providing suggestions or assistance in developing these materials.

Tracy Harrison, Wendy Kanter, and students at the Santa Barbara Charter School

Barnabas Hughes

Marc Jackson

Rachel Jackson

Natalie Lyman

Zoe Pasternack-Marsh (a special thanks for the creation of the "bunny" on the cover)

Lynda Wormell

Erica Zacarias and her students at Darby Elementary School (Los Angeles)

Executive Editor: ***Catherine Anderson***
Project Editor: ***ToniAnn Guadagnoli***
Project Sponsor: ***Merle Silverman***
Copy Editor: ***Cheryl Turner***
Production/Manufacturing Director: ***Janet Yearian***
Production/Manufacturing Coordinator: ***Joan Lee***
Design Director: ***Phyllis Aycock***
Design Manager: ***Jeff Kelly***
Text and Cover Design: ***Don Taka***
Composition and Line Art: ***Alan Noyes***

Cuisenaire Company of America
10 Bank Street
White Plains, NY 10602-5026
Customer Service: 800-237-3142

Printed in the United States of America.

Order Number 034717
ISBN 1-57452-249-3

1 2 3 4 5 6 7 8 9 10-ML-03 02 01 00 99

This Book Is Printed
On Recycled Paper

Table of Contents

Introduction and History

Tangram Blocks™ is a collection of 14 blocks representing a double set of tangrams in three-dimensional form. The blocks were developed from the original seven tangrams: five triangles, a square, and a parallelogram, all usually of a single color. Thus a new set of puzzles has been created from a very old puzzle.

The multicolored Tangram Blocks include ten triangular prisms, two cubes, and two parallelepipeds. The colorful blocks promote stimulating three-dimensional challenges for all age groups and include forming unusual patterns and designs. Students use higher-order thinking skills to arrange the geometric solids and analyze their characteristics.

Tangram Blocks provide in three dimensions all the activities flat tangrams accomplish in two dimensions. By separating the set of 14 Tangram Blocks into two matching sets of seven blocks, and with appropriate changes in terminology from two to three dimensions, the exercises suggested for the flat tangrams can be carried out with Tangram Blocks.

All the activities in this book have been designed to heighten the students' sense of spatial relationships using the three-dimensional blocks. In these activities, students

- explore block characteristics,
- develop appropriate terminology,
- develop problem-solving skills,
- find different combinations of blocks to build congruent figures, and
- record simple solutions to selected block problems.

History of Tangrams

In *The Eighth Book of Tan* written by Sam Loyd and published in 1902 (Dover reprint 1968 with an introduction by Peter Van Note), the author attempted to convince puzzle fans that tangrams had existed in the Chinese culture for more than four thousand years. His explanation, while elaborate and entertaining, later proved to be purely fictional, lacking substantive historical evidence. The seven-piece set of flat tangrams was probably a creation of a Chinese puzzle maker in the late 1700s. One of the early tangram enthusiasts was Lewis Carroll. He owned the book *The Fashionable Chinese Puzzle* (New York, 1817), which may have sparked his intrigue with the seven pieces that can be arranged in so many shapes. Even Edgar Allen Poe had an intricately carved set of ivory tangrams, which were packaged as two layers in a carved ivory box.

The geometric relationships among the flat tangrams opened the doors to an abundance of instructional and recreational mathematics. Beginning in 1959, Martin Gardner wrote extensively about tangrams in *Scientific American*. Further, he summarized both historical and geometric aspects of tangrams in *Time Travel and Other Mathematical Bewilderments* (Freeman, 1988), chapters 2 and 3. In the 1960s, mathematics education emphasized using manipulative materials for hands-on instruction. Whenever appropriate, tangrams entered the classroom as a learning tool. In 1971, Dale Seymour authored and published *Tangramath*. It is a book of activity pages for students of all grades to discover patterns and construct two-dimensional geometric shapes.

Selected Curriculum Standards of the National Council of Teachers of Mathematics

Listed below are the selected curriculum standards with which the activities from each section comply.*

	Block Basics	Puzzles and Designs
Problem Solving	2–4, 14–17	80–81
Communication	10	94–100
Reasoning	5–9, 11–13, 18	82–94
Number Sense	2–4, 14	94–100
Geometry and Spatial Sense	2–18	80–100
Patterns and Relations	5–9, 11, 13	94–100

	Block Figures
Problem Solving	20, 24, 26, 35–37
Communication	30, 32, 34–44
Reasoning	21–23, 25, 27–29, 31, 33, 38–44
Geometry and Spatial Sense	20–44

	Block Buildings	Symmetry Patterns
Problem Solving	46–47	63–78
Communication	46–61	64–78
Reasoning	48–61	64–78
Geometry and Spatial Sense	46–61	63–78
Patterns and Relations		63–78

*The activities are listed by page numbers, not activity numbers.

Chapter 1

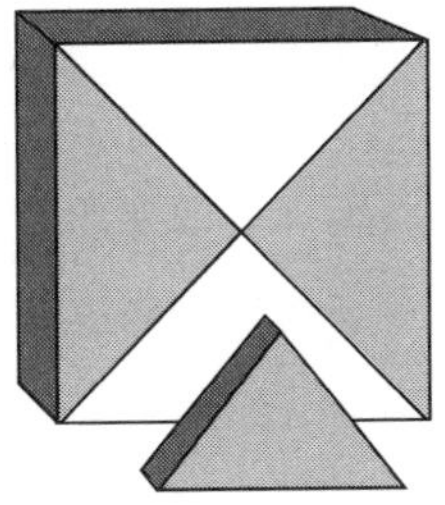

Block Basics

Overview

In this section students become familiar with the characteristics of the Tangram Blocks by comparing and classifying them. The activities include explorations with the following:

- the blocks' colors, shapes, and sizes
- the blocks' geometric names
- the number and shape of the faces on each block
- the relationship of the small triangular prisms to the other blocks
- how triangular prisms form other blocks and solids

You may notice the following while observing students working on this section.

- Students use very creative ways to stack and organize the blocks.
- Students may use the blocks to fill the outlines so that the top surface appears to have mountains and valleys and is not flat. These arrangements, however, are not the focus of this book.
- Most students quickly realize the differences between the sizes of the triangular prisms.
- Some very young students may have difficulty finding the square side on the parallelepiped.
- In the beginning, some students will give up trying to fit a specific block onto a figure. Replacing it with a different but congruent block, they will successfully make the match.

Before you begin the first activity, give students some instruction on how to use the activity pages. Each one has a shape drawn on it (except for Activities 4 and 17). In this section, the outlines are actual size—students are to set their blocks on the shapes so that the edges of the blocks fit within the edges of the drawing. In later sections, some activity pages show a reduced outline of the shape students are to create on their desks.

Exploring the Blocks

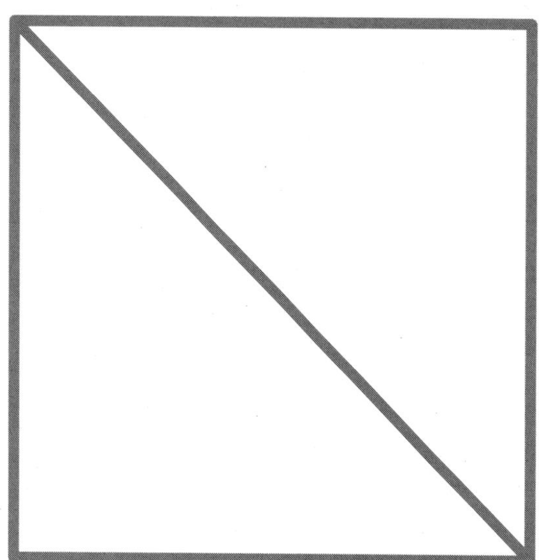

Build up.

How many stories high? __________

How many blocks? __________

Exploring the Blocks

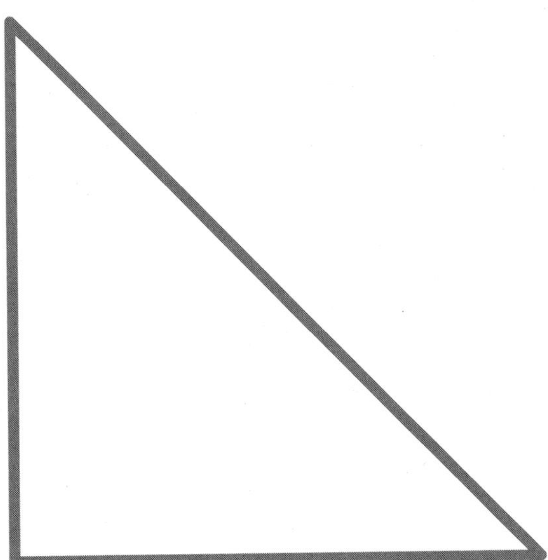

Build up.

How many stories high? ___________

How many blocks? ___________

Exploring the Blocks

Build up.

How many stories high? ___________

How many blocks? ___________

Build up.

How many stories high? ___________

How many blocks? ___________

Sorting Blocks

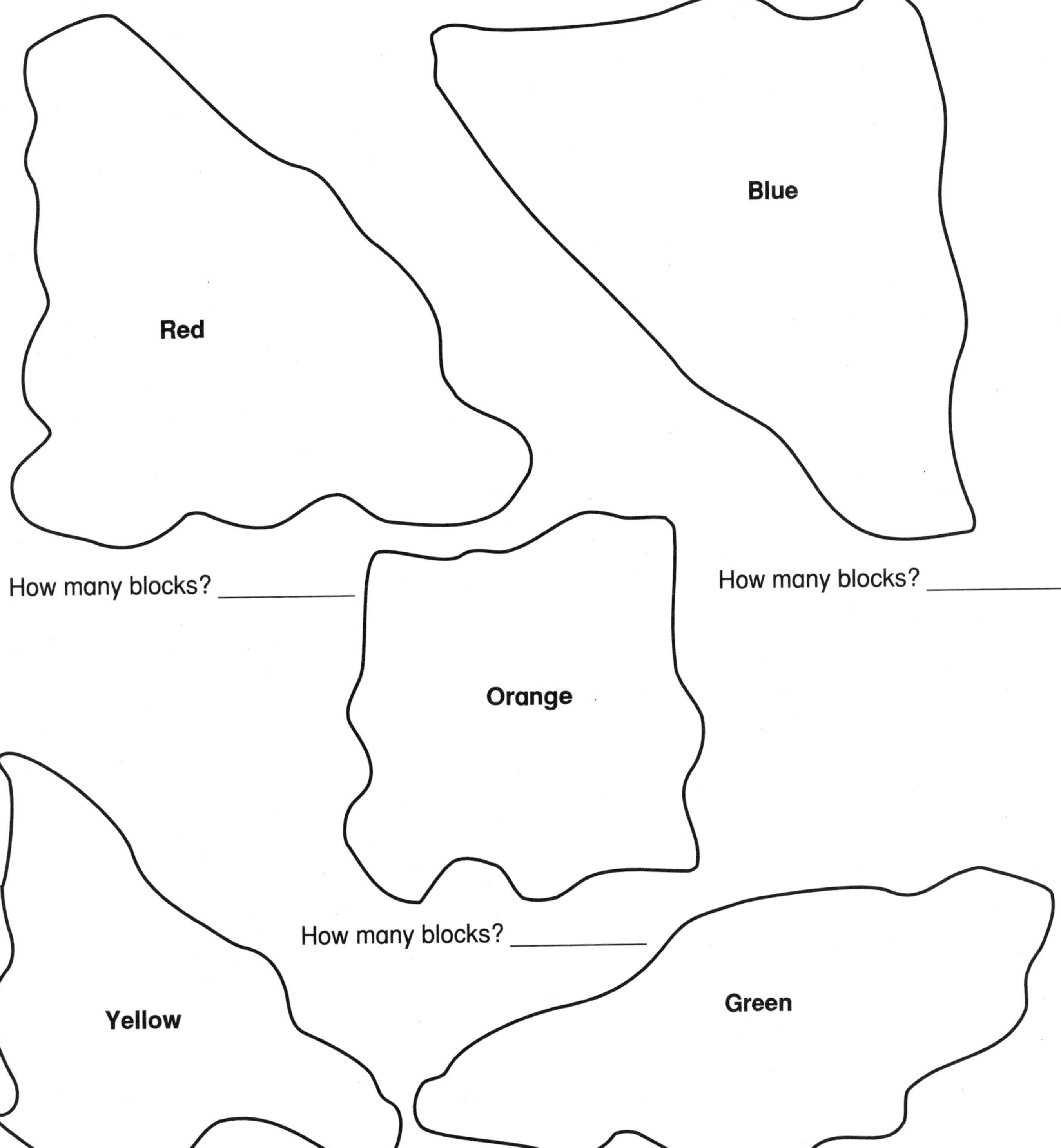

How many blocks? ____________

How many blocks? ____________

How many blocks? ____________

How many blocks? ____________

How many blocks? ____________

Sorting Blocks

Match a Tangram Block to each shape.

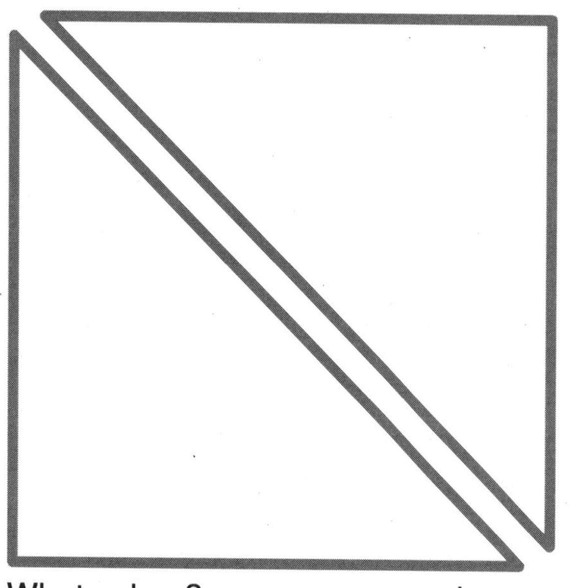

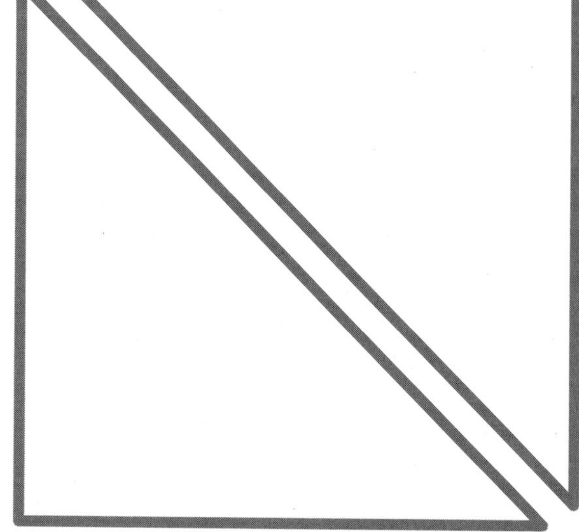

What colors? __________ and __________

What color? __________

What colors? __________ and __________

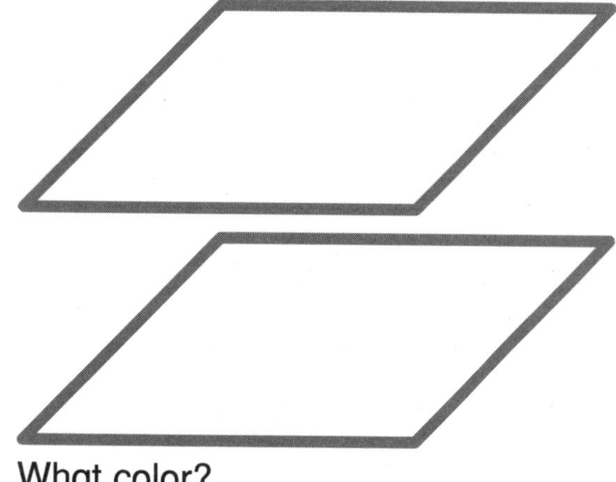

What color? __________

What color? __________

Sorting Blocks

Match a Tangram Block to each square shape.

Orange

Orange

Red

Red

Blue

Blue

Green

Green

Sorting Blocks

Match a Tangram Block to each rectangular shape.

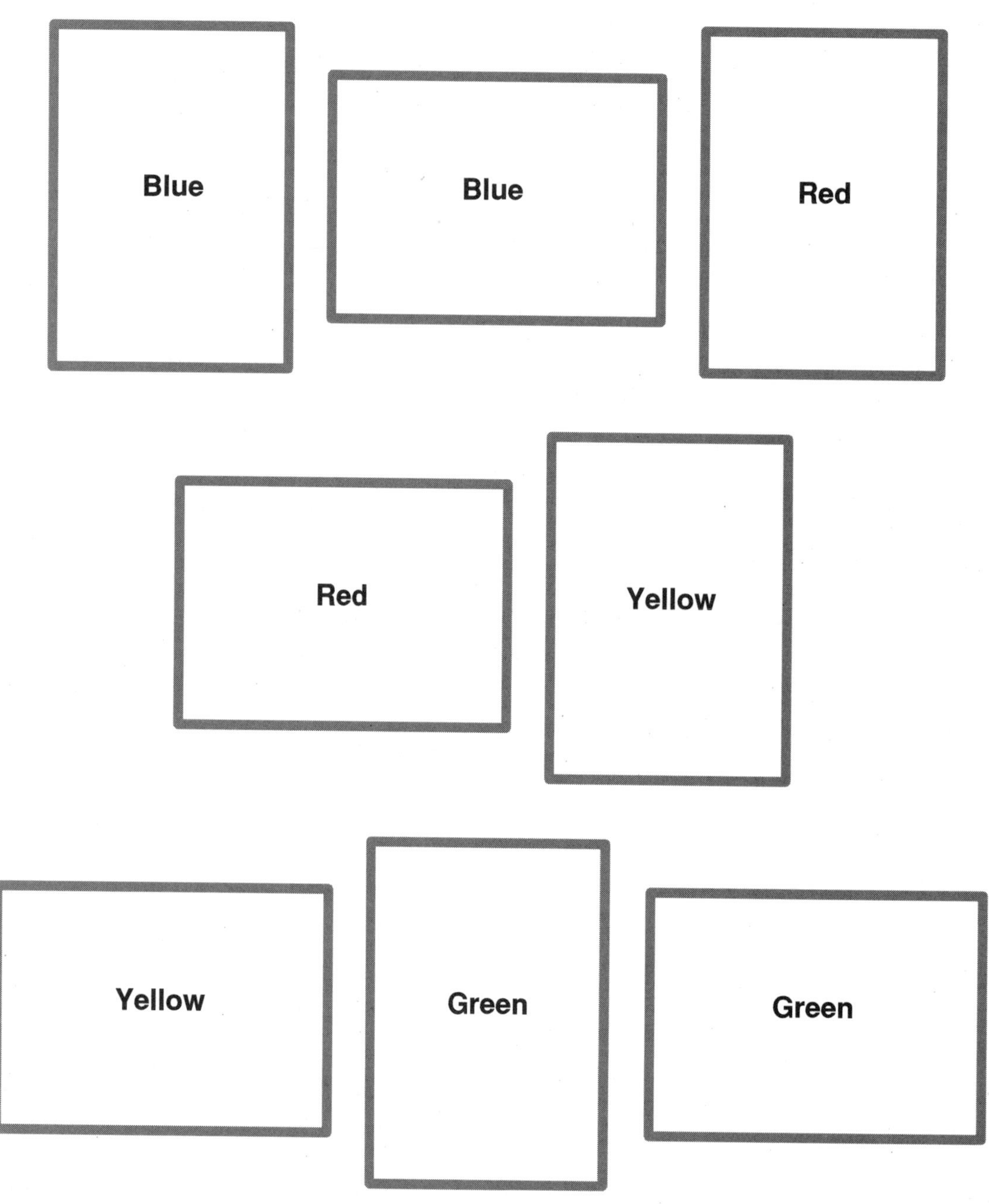

Sorting Blocks

Match a Tangram Block to each rectangular shape.

Yellow

Yellow

Blue

Red

Red

Blue

Sorting Blocks

Which colors of Tangram Blocks go with each shape?

Sorting Blocks

Match a Tangram Block to each shape.

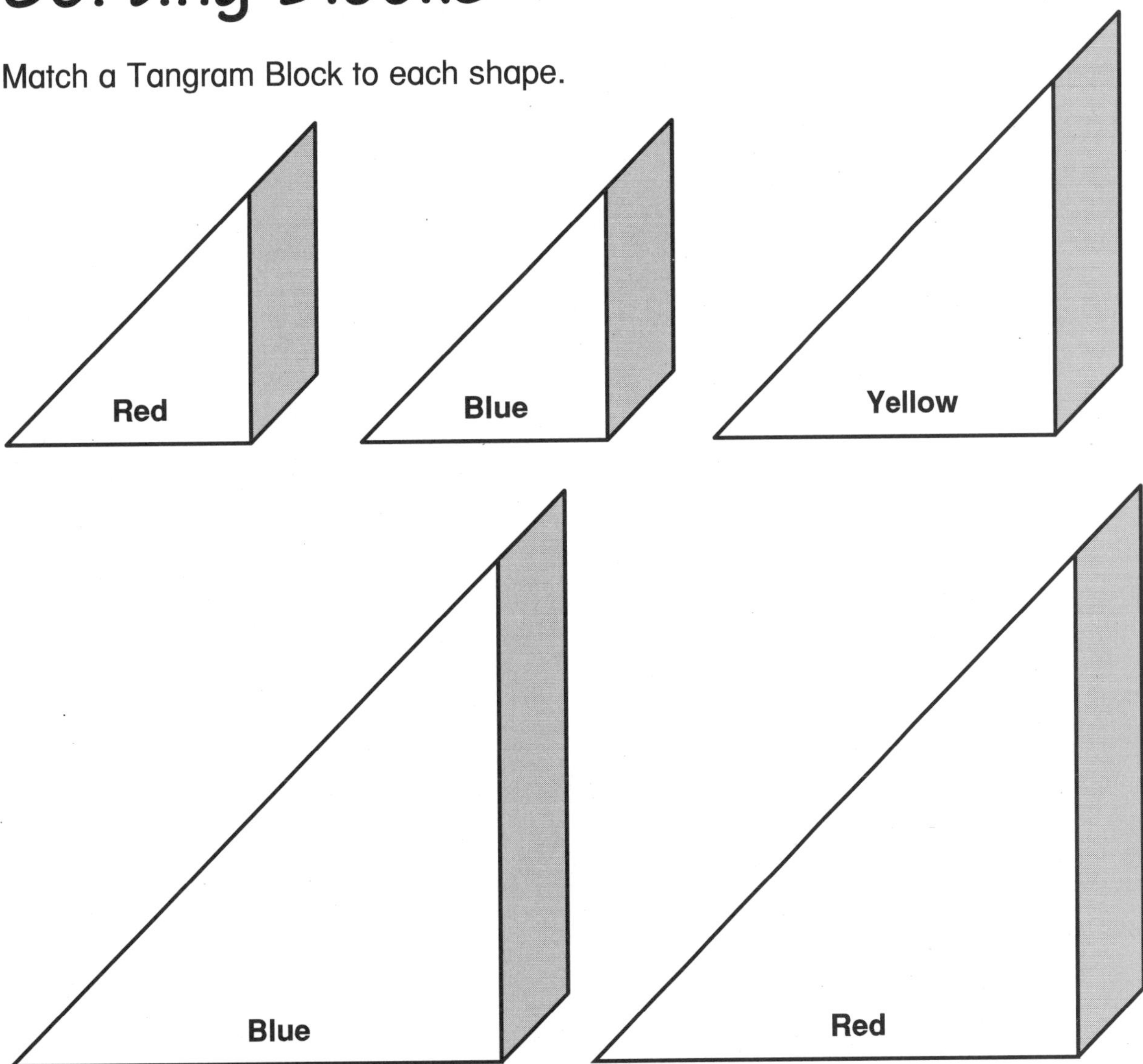

These blocks are called *triangular prisms* because two opposite sides (faces) are triangles.

Are they all the same size? ___________

What colors are the small triangular prisms? ___________ and ___________

What color is the medium-size triangular prism? ___________

What colors are the large triangular prisms? ___________ and ___________

How many sides (faces) does each triangular prism have? ___________

Using the Blocks

Match a Tangram Block to each shape.

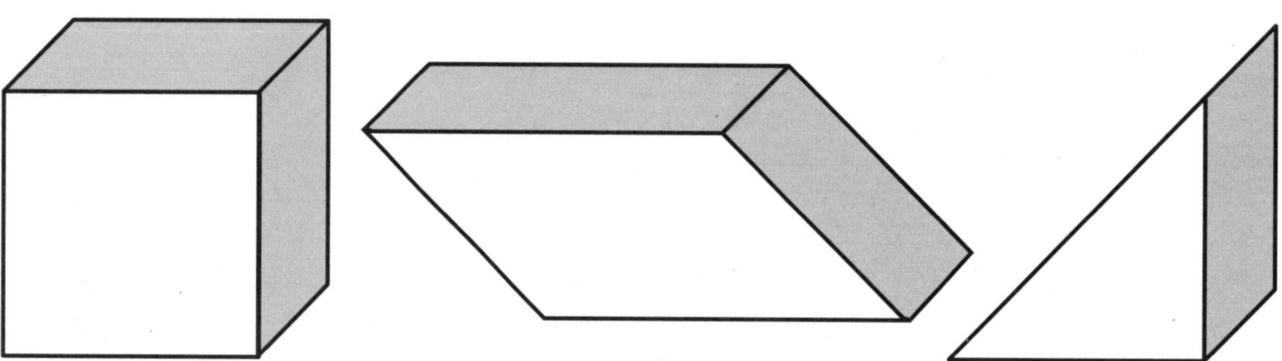

The orange block is called a *cube* because all its sides (faces) have the same shape and size.

How many sides does the cube have? __________

How many different-shaped faces does the cube have? __________

The green block is called a *parallelepiped.*

How many sides (faces) does the parallelepiped have? __________

How many different-shaped faces does the parallelepiped have? __________

Look at the triangular prism.

How many sides (faces) does the triangular prism have? __________

How many different-shaped faces does the triangular prism have? __________

Using the Blocks

1. Use two small triangular prisms (STP) to build one medium triangular prism (MTP).

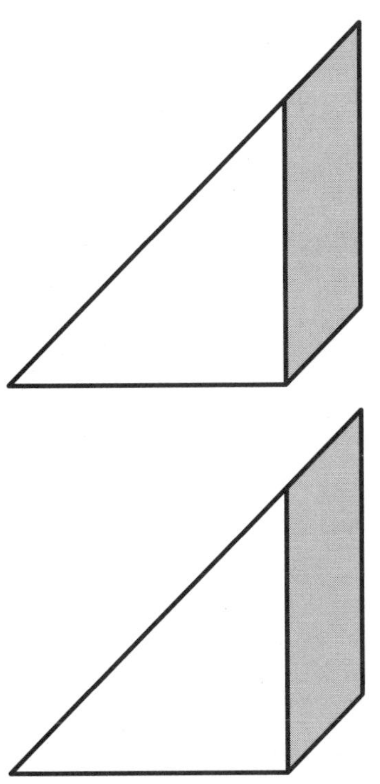

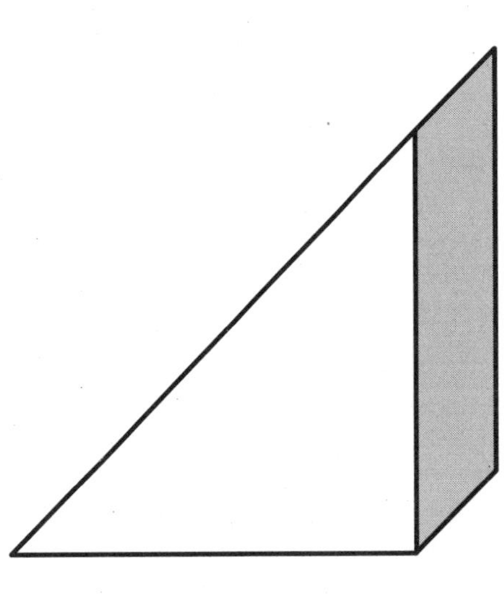

2. Use two medium triangular prisms (MTP) to build one large triangular prism (LTP).

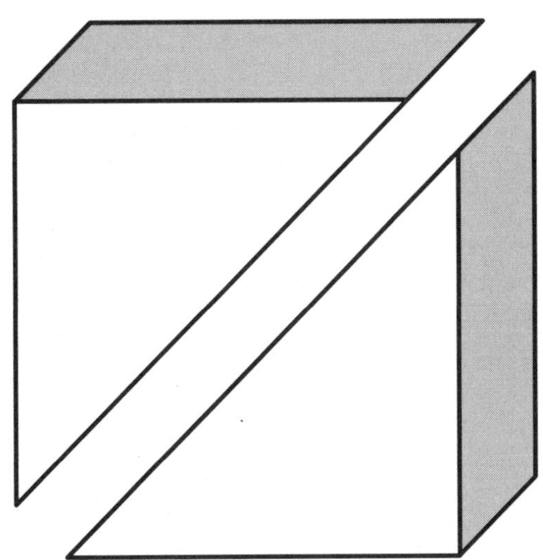

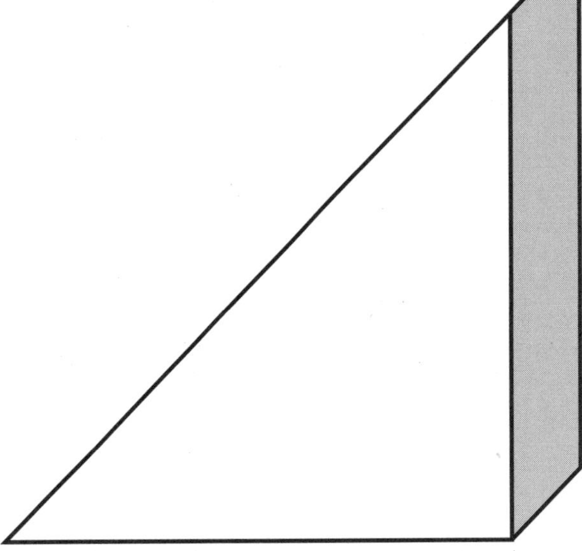

Using the Blocks

Build a jumbo triangular prism using four large triangular prisms,

or three large triangular prisms *and* two medium triangular prisms,

or three large triangular prisms *and* one medium triangular prism *and* two small triangular prisms,

or three large triangular prisms *and* four small triangular prisms,

or two large triangular prisms *and* two medium triangular prisms *and* four small triangular prisms.

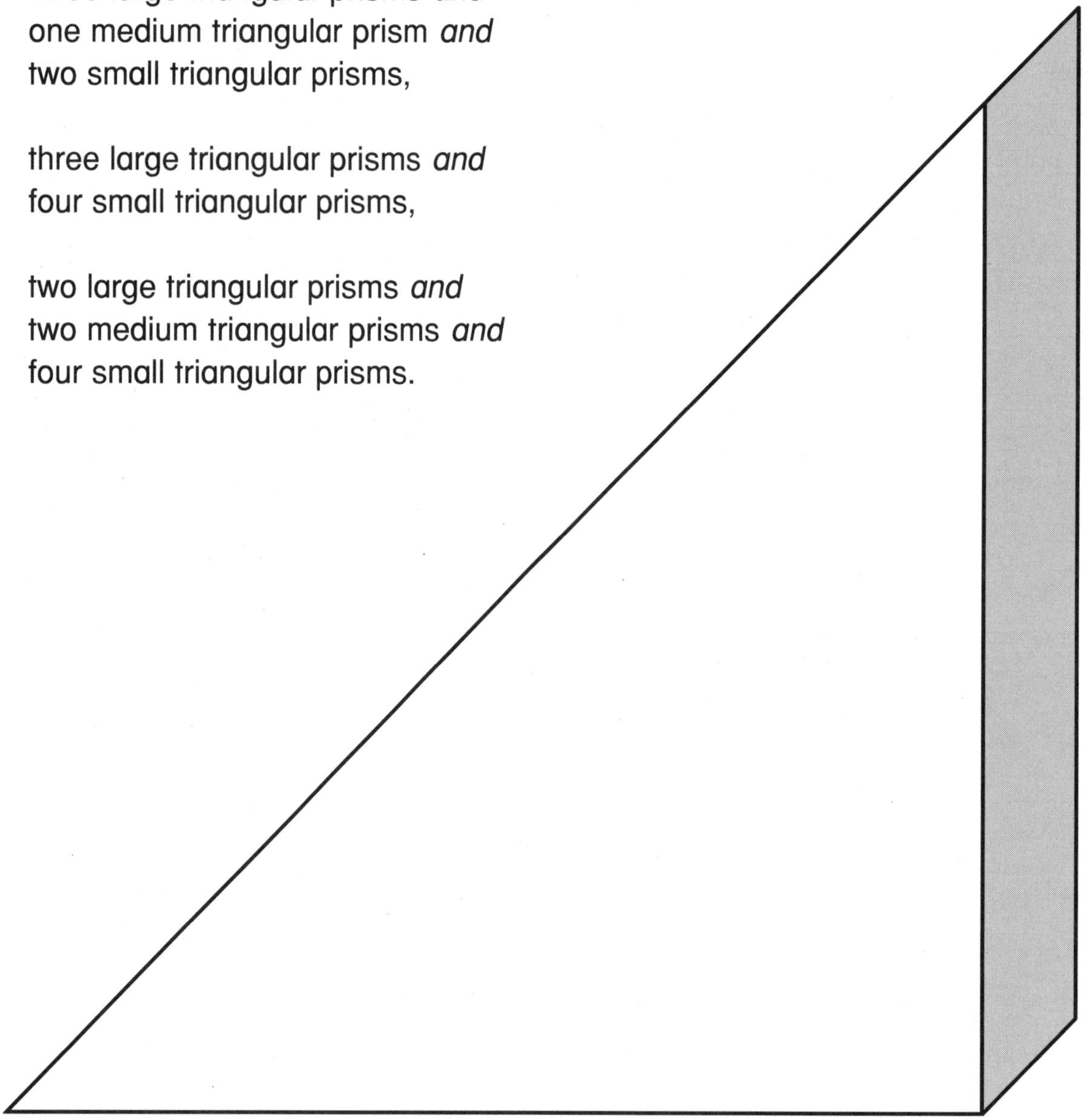

Using the Blocks

1. Build a cube using two small triangular prisms.

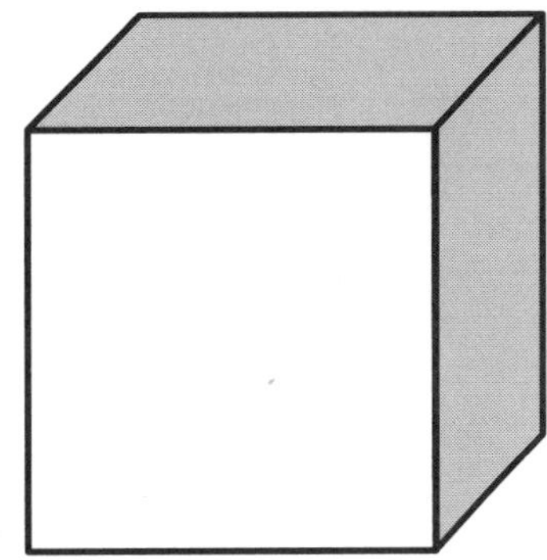

2. Build a large cube using four large triangular prisms.

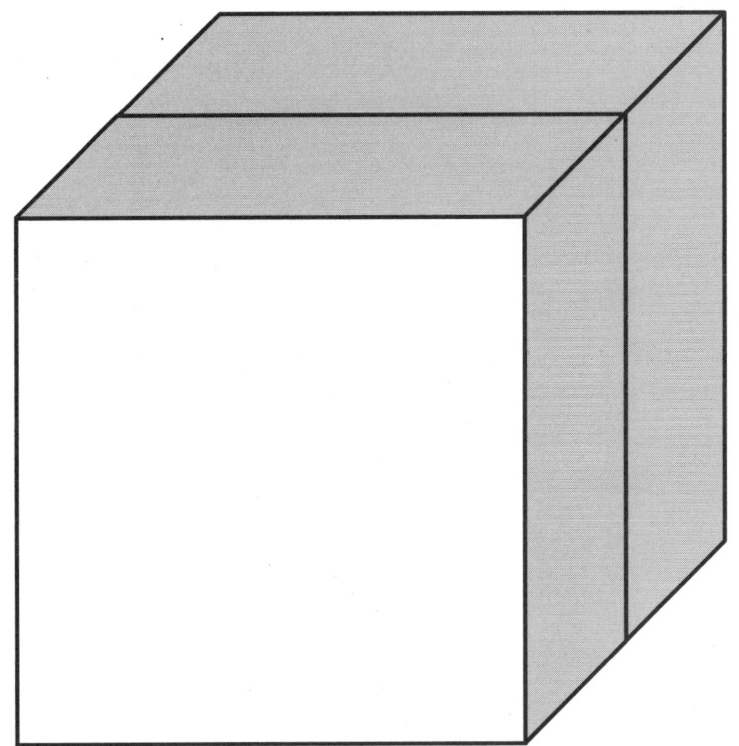

Challenge!

3. Build the same large cube but this time using
   two cubes *and*
   two parallelepipeds *and*
   two medium triangular prisms *and*
   four small triangular prisms.

Using the Blocks

1. Build a parallelepiped using two small triangular prisms.

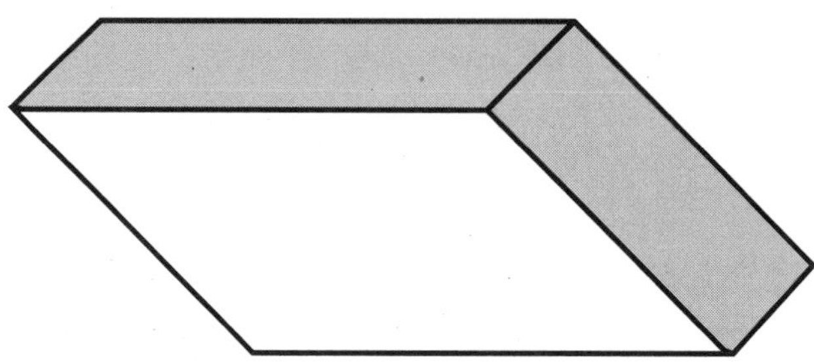

2. Build a larger parallelepiped using two parallelepipeds,

   or two medium triangular prisms,

   or four small triangular prisms,

   or one parallelepiped *and* two small triangular prisms,

   or one medium triangular prism *and* two small triangular prisms.

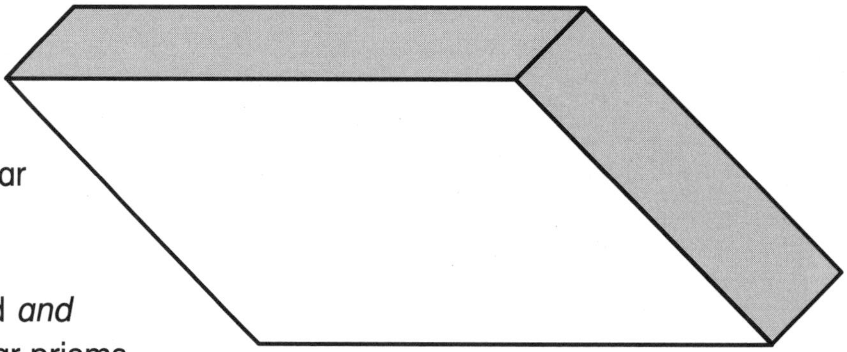

Using the Blocks

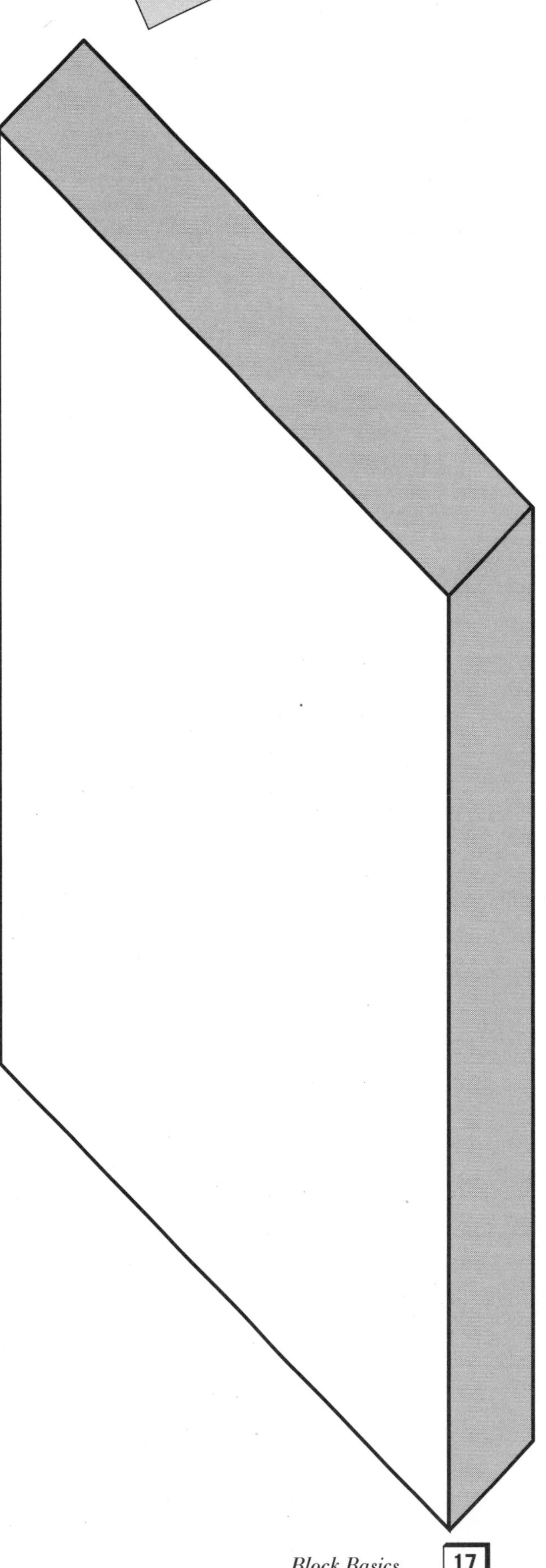

Build a jumbo parallelepiped using four large triangular prisms,

or two large triangular prisms *and*
two medium triangular prisms *and*
two parallelepipeds,

or two cubes *and*
two parallelepipeds *and*
two medium triangular prisms *and*
four small triangular prisms.

Challenge!
Find another way to build this jumbo parallelepiped.

Using the Blocks

Each of the Tangram Blocks is a type of polyhedron made up of these parts.

FACES	flat sides called *polygons*
EDGES	line segments where **two** faces or polygons meet
VERTICES	the points where **three** edges meet

This cube shows these parts:

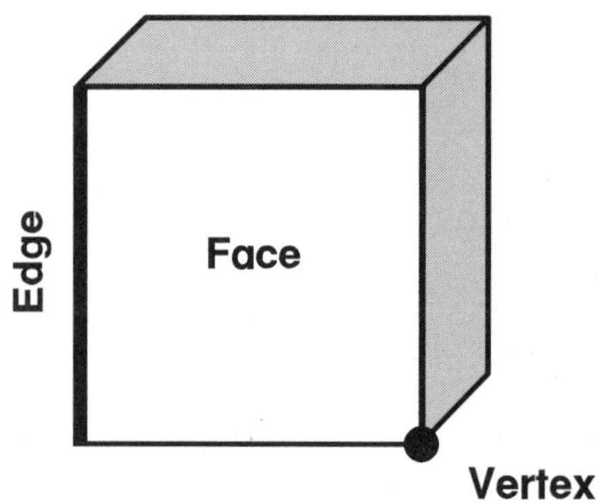

Complete the chart below by describing each of the block pieces.

Name	Color(s)	Number of Faces	Number of Edges	Number of Vertices
Cube	Orange	6	12	8
Small Triangular Prism				
Medium Triangular Prism				
Large Triangular Prism				
Parallelepiped				

Chapter 2

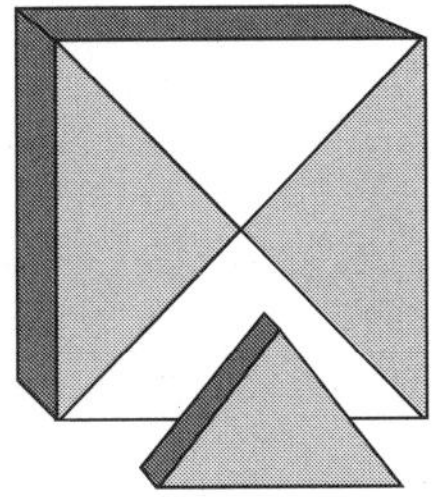

Block Figures

Overview

In this section, students continue to develop visual discrimination by combining Tangram Blocks to form various shapes. This increases their ability to recognize objects in space. Most of the shapes they will form will be one-level high. Students do the following:

- Form very simple shapes from the four small triangular prisms.
- Use two each of two different blocks.
- Use five blocks of three different kinds.
- Rebuild the same figure with different blocks, several ways.
- Record *selected* solutions on dot paper.

Caution: not all combinations of blocks can be recorded easily on dot paper. An explanation of the complete graphic representation can be found in the authors' book, *Tangram Blocks Activities, Grades 5–10.*

- Build and record three-dimensional numerals (0–9) one-level high, using a variety of blocks.

You may notice the following while observing students working on this section.

- Students quickly develop a sense of matching congruent faces to build various figures.
- Recording solutions does not depend on grade level. Some first-grade students are able to record their solutions easily, while some third-grade students require assistance.

Note: The answers to Activities 11 and 15 can be recorded on Appendix 2. The answers to Activities 16–25 can be recorded on Appendix 1.

Simple Shapes

Use four small triangular prisms to fill each outline.

A

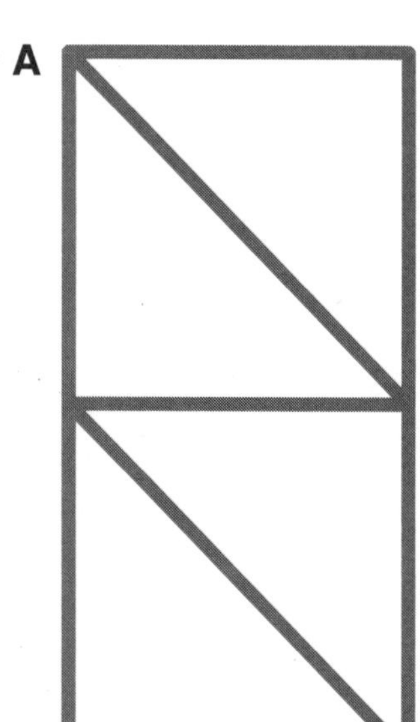

C

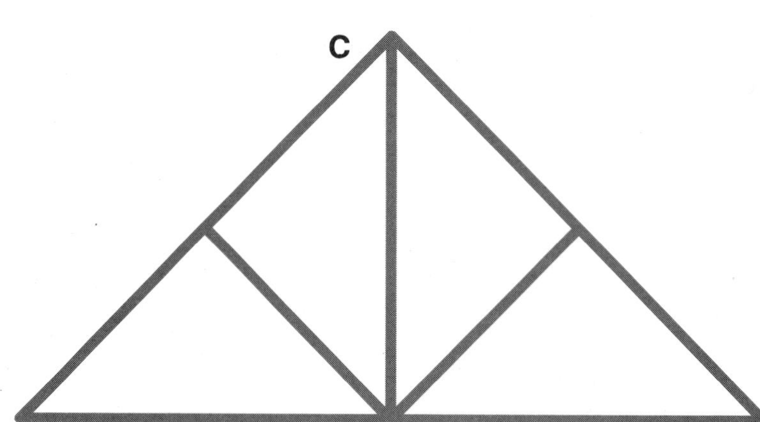

B

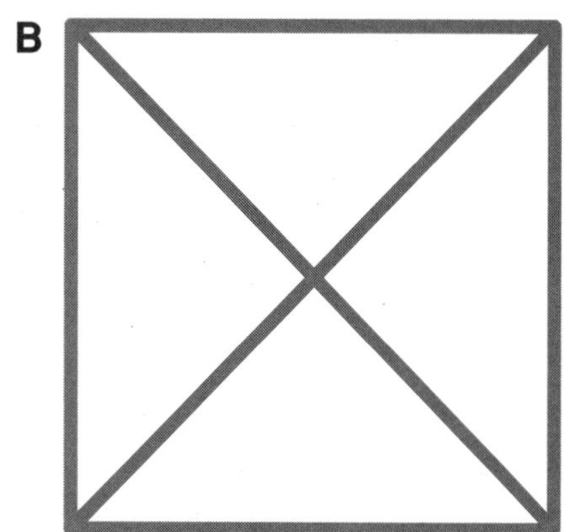

D

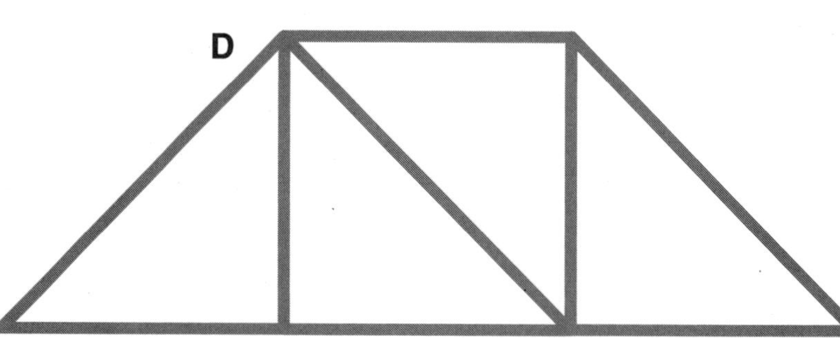

Simple Shapes

Use four small triangular prisms to fill each outline.

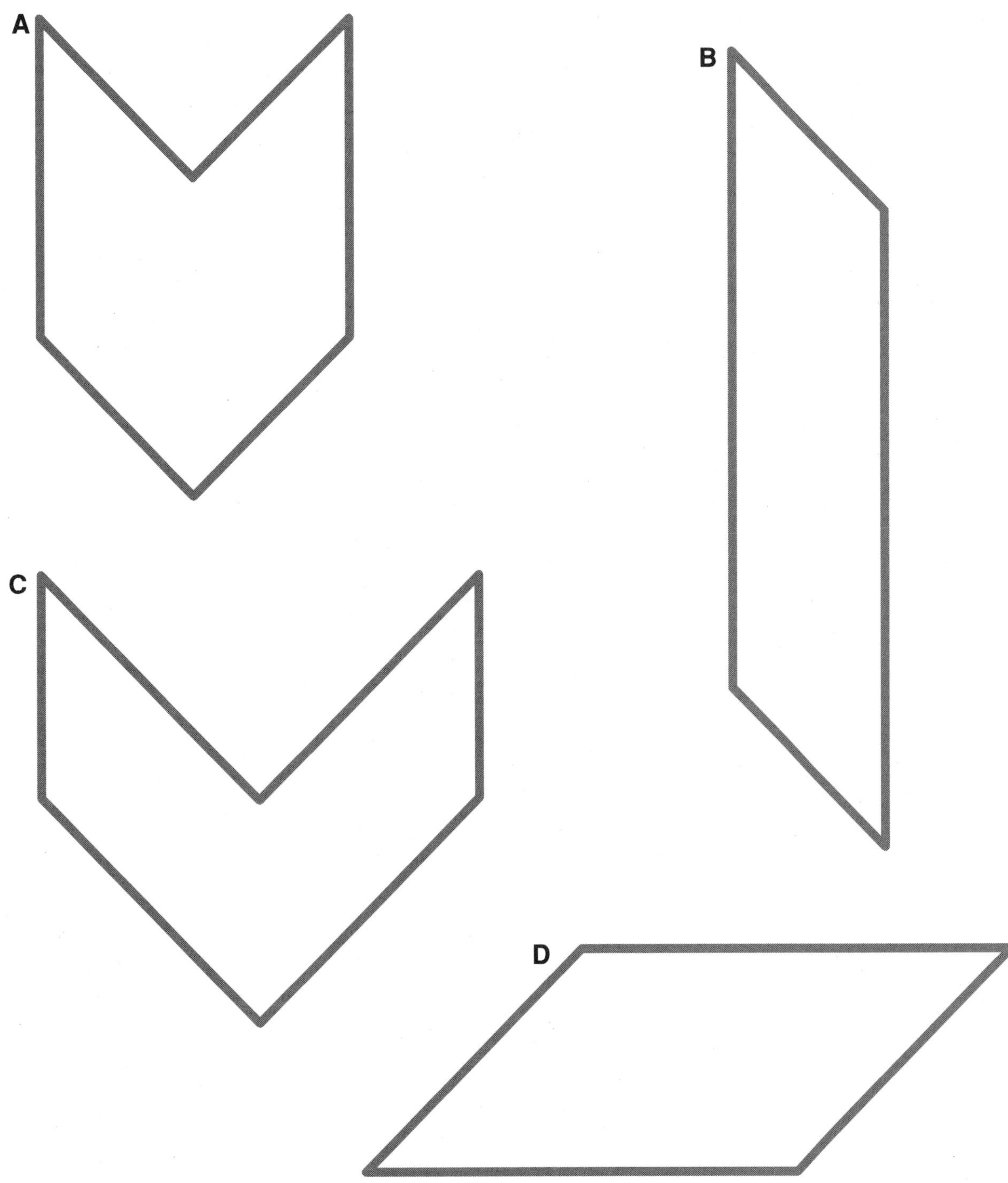

Simple Shapes

Use two cubes and two parallelepipeds to fill each outline.

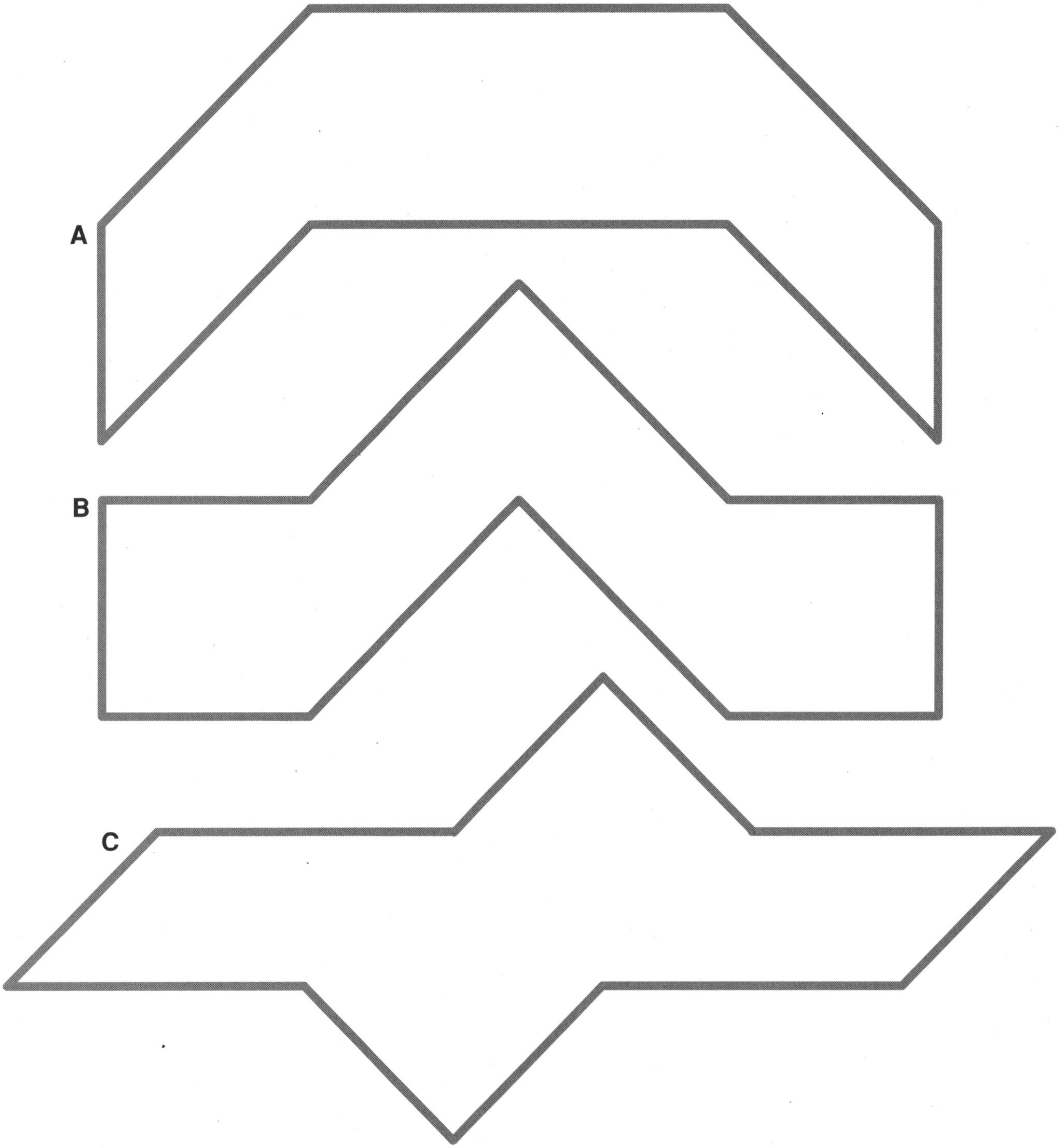

A

B

C

Simple Shapes

Use two cubes and two parallelepipeds to fill each outline.

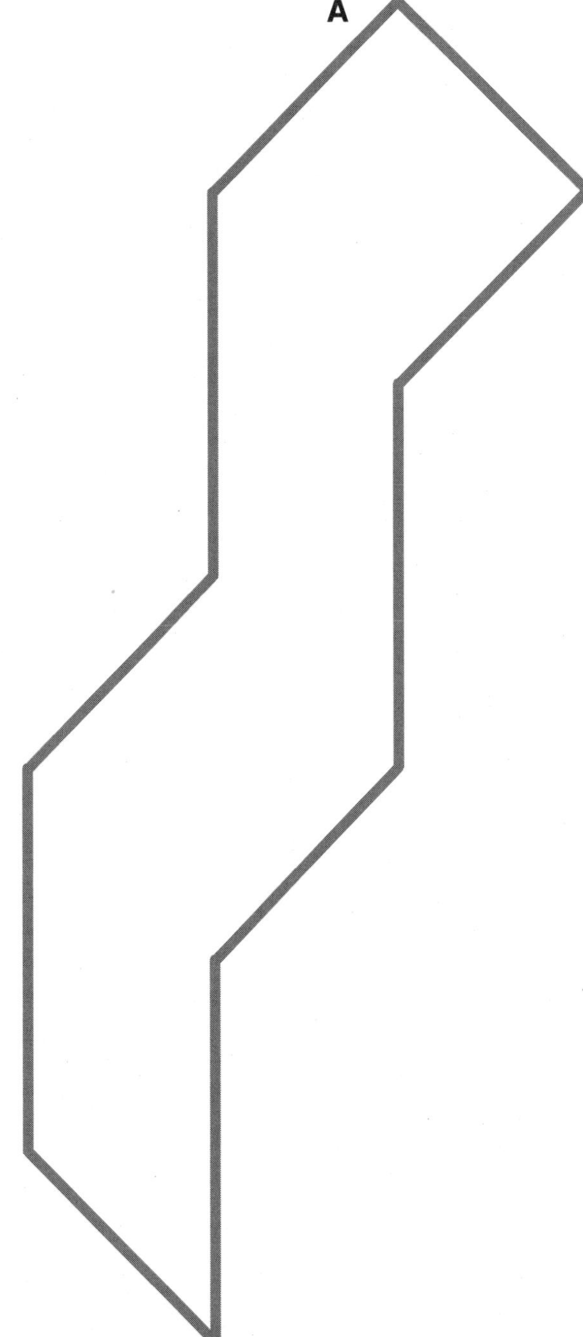

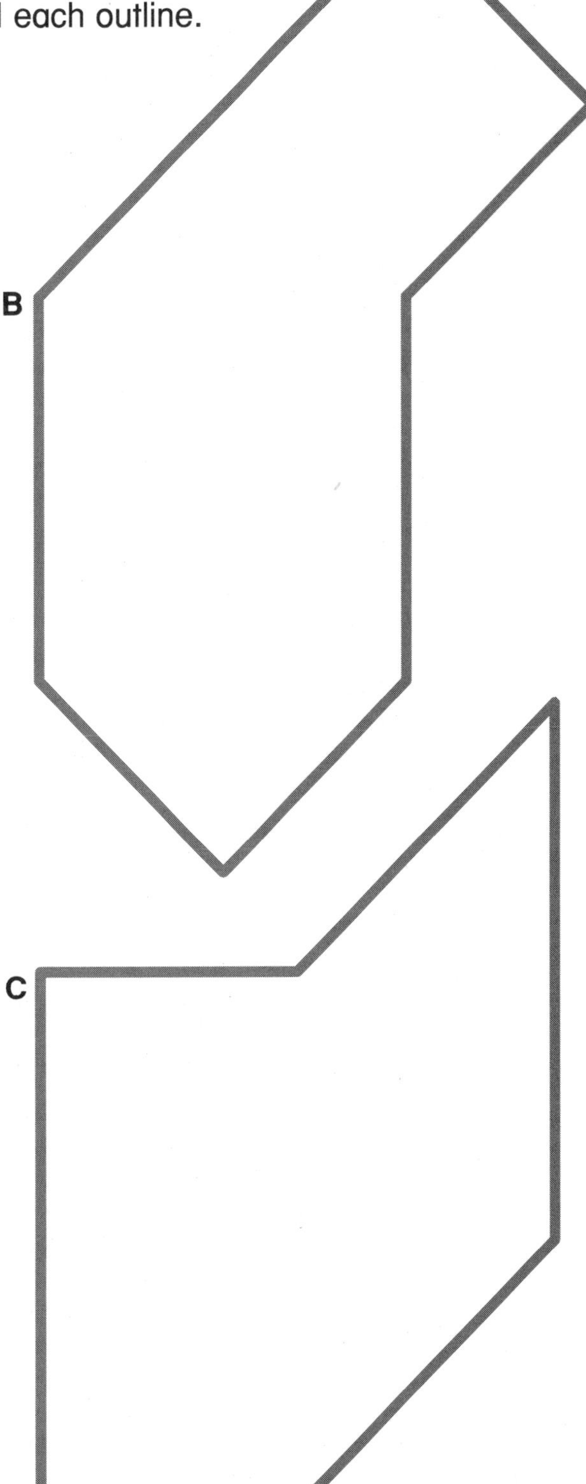

Complex Shapes

Use two medium triangular prisms and two parallelepipeds to fill each outline.

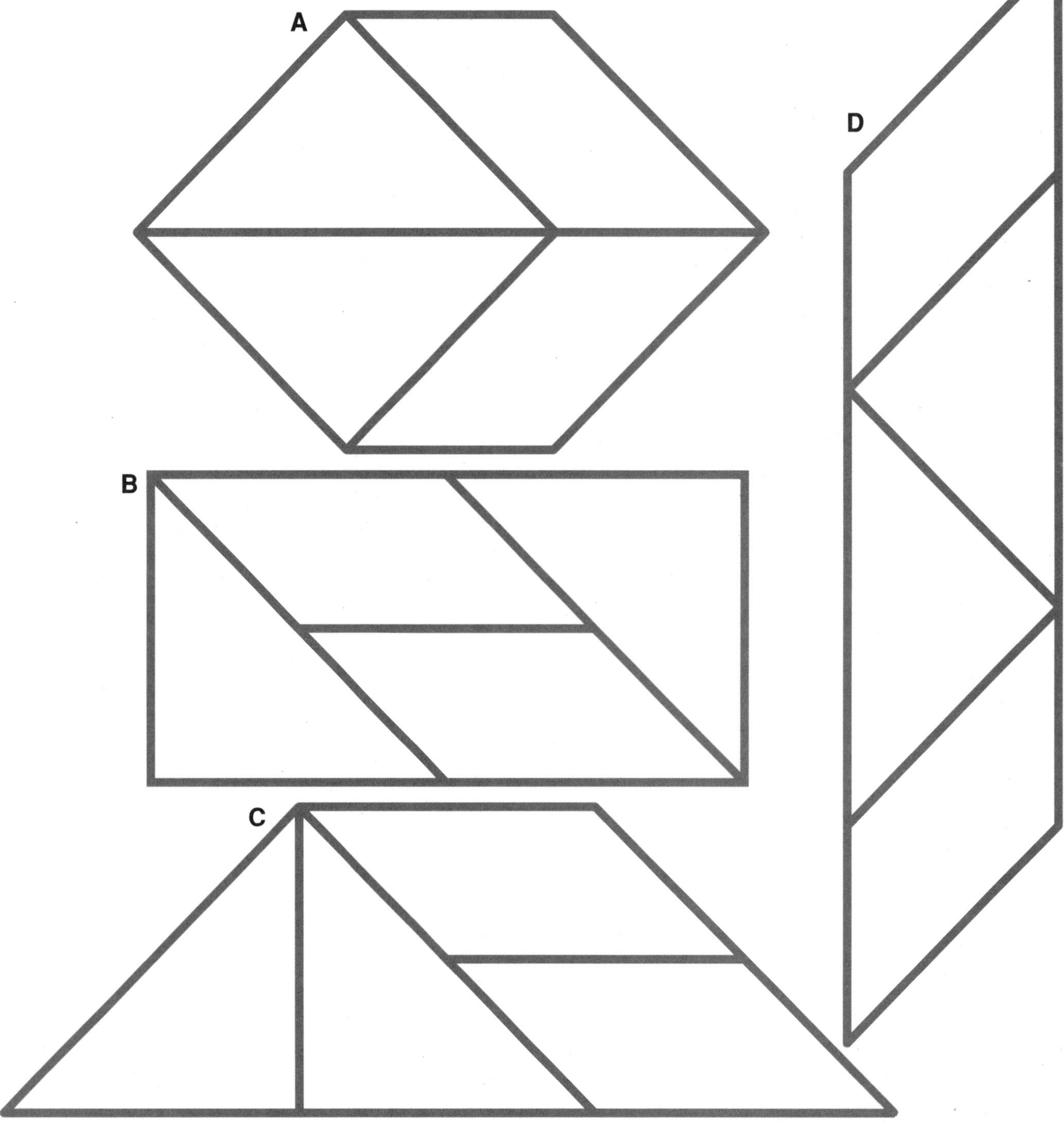

Complex Shapes

1. Use two medium triangular prisms and two parallelepipeds to fill outlines A, B, and C.

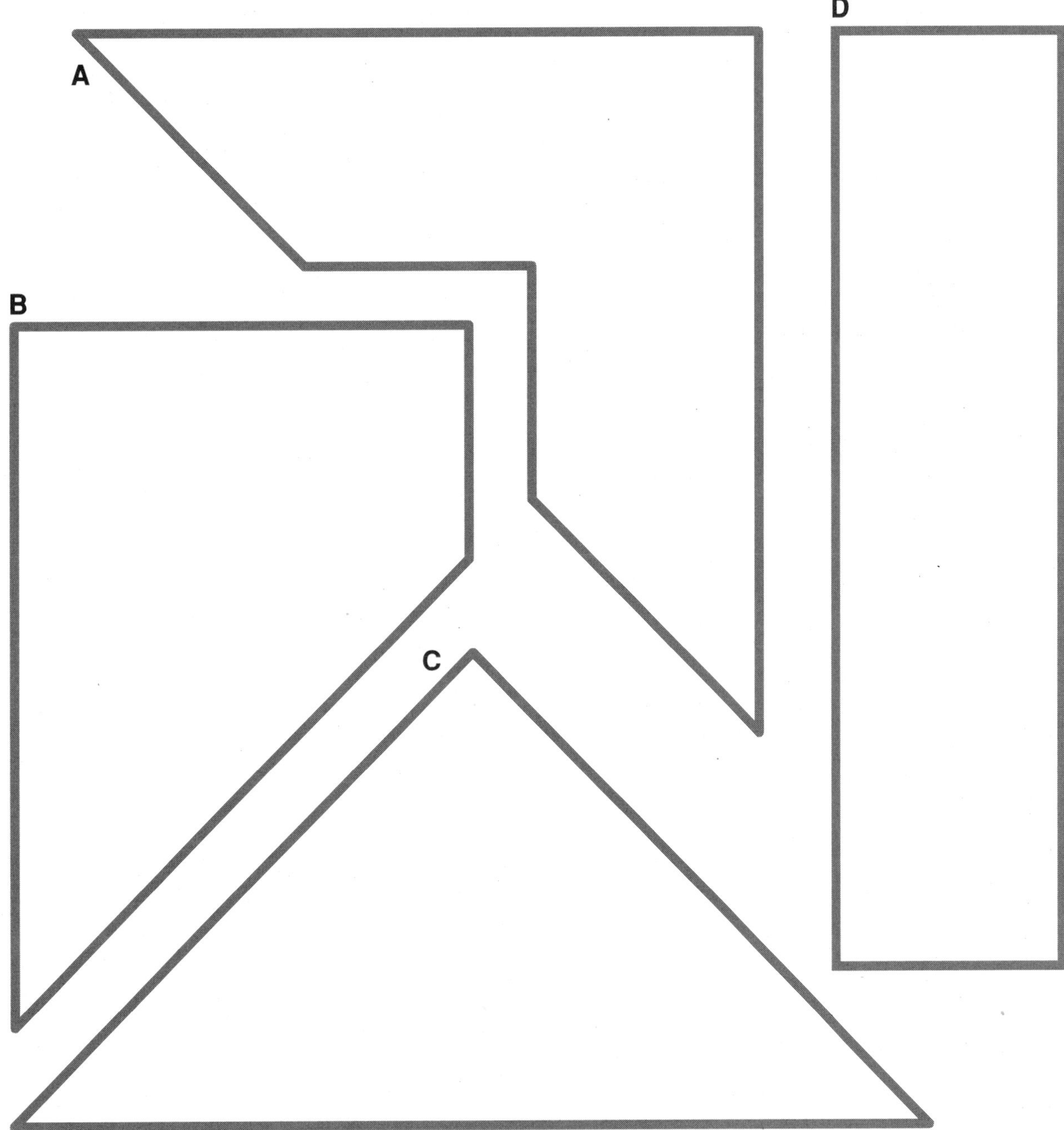

2. Use the block figure on outline C to cover outline D. Note: D will not be flat on top.

Complex Shapes

Use one cube, two small triangular prisms, and two parallelepipeds to fill each outline.

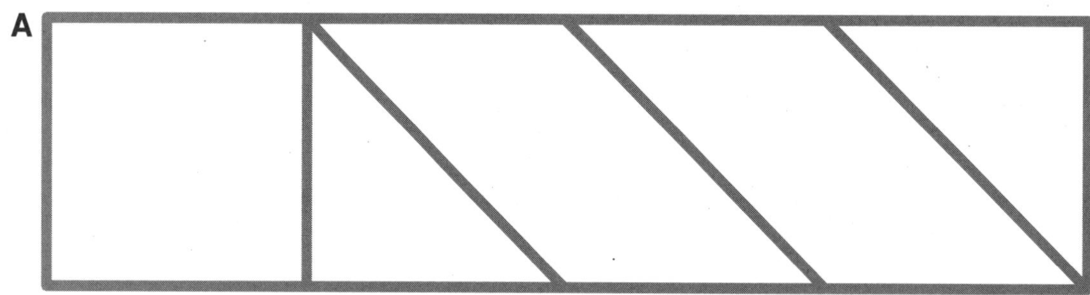

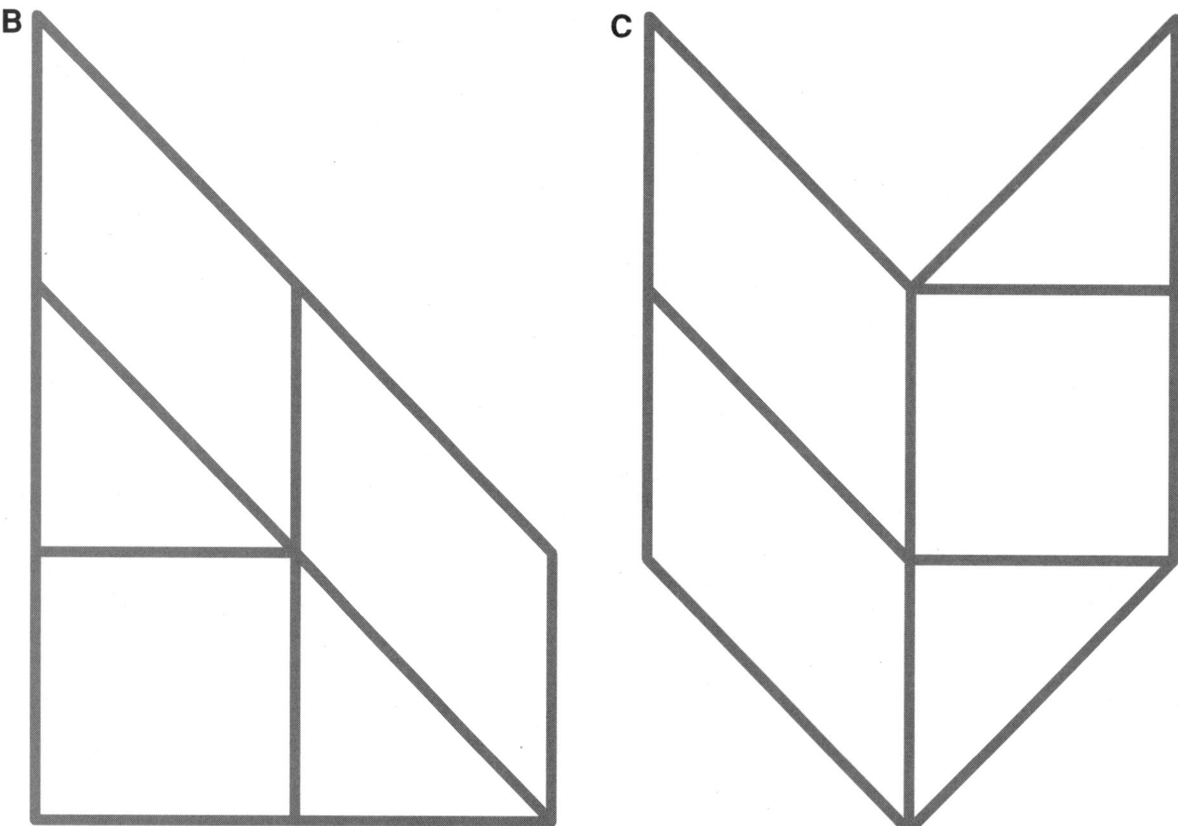

Complex Shapes

Use one cube, two small triangular prisms, and two parallelepipeds to fill each outline.

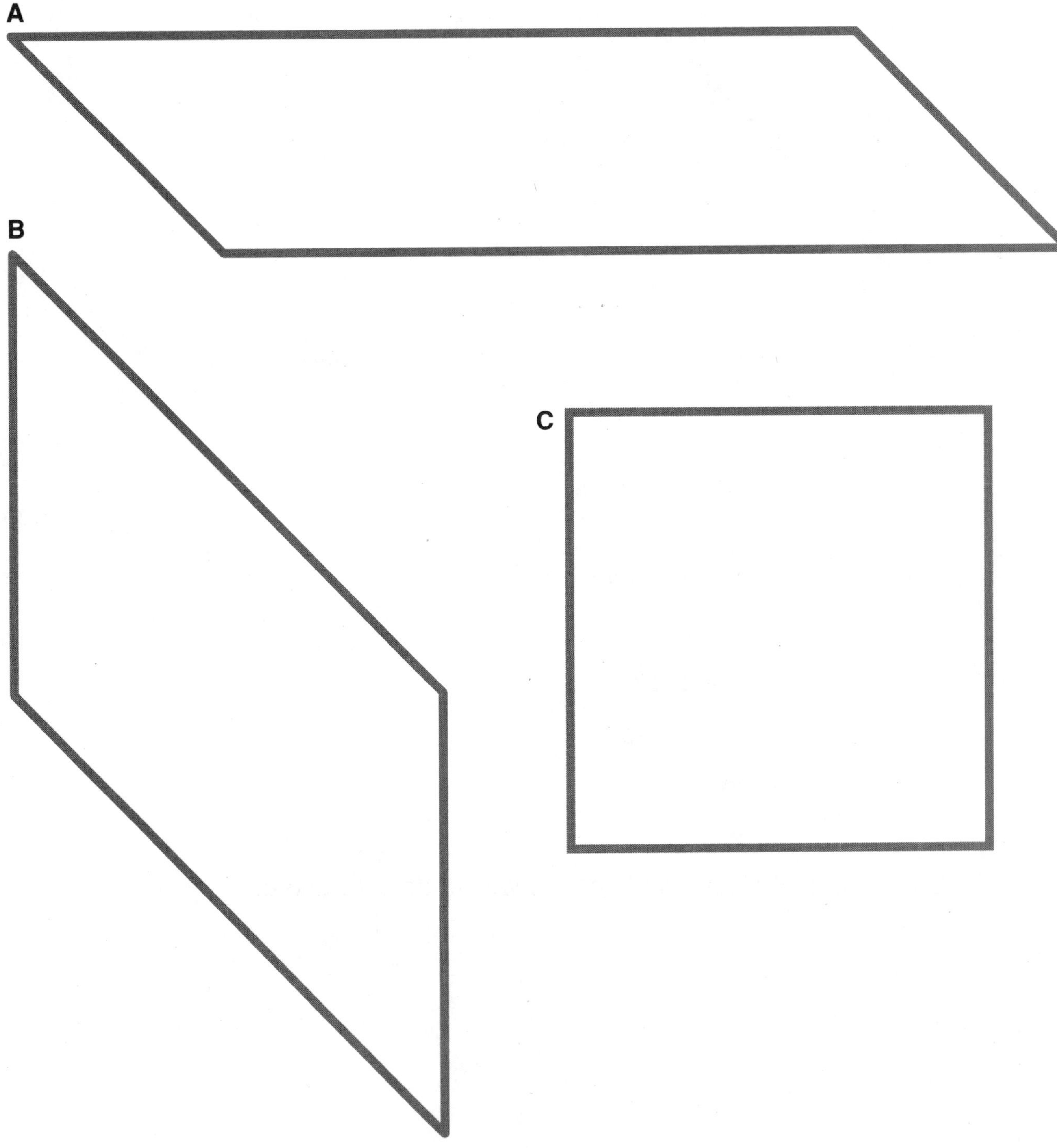

Triangular Prisms

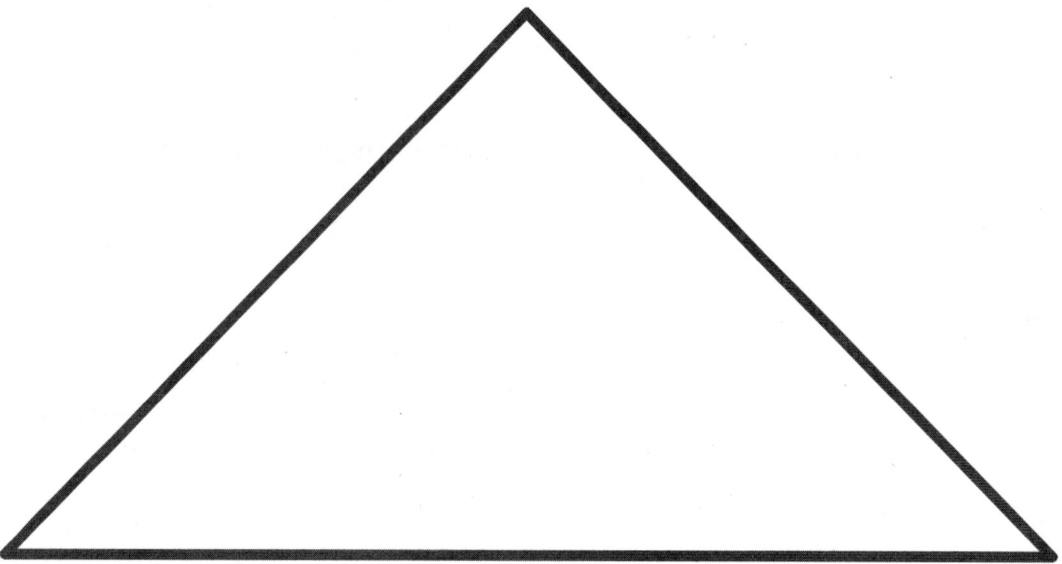

1. Fill the outline using
   a. two Tangram Blocks.
   b. three blocks.
   c. four blocks.
   d. five blocks.
   e. six blocks.

2. Using different blocks, find another way to do c, d, and e.

Pentagonal Prisms

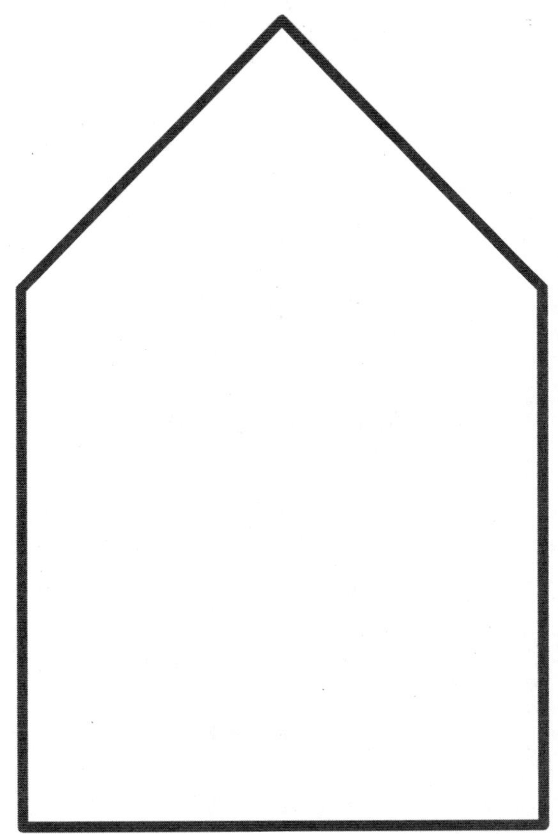

1. Fill the outline using
   - **a.** three Tangram Blocks.
   - **b.** four blocks.
   - **c.** five blocks.
   - **d.** six blocks.
   - **e.** seven blocks.
2. Using different blocks, find another way to do b, c, d, and e.

Pentagonal Prisms

Here are pictures of how the Tangram Blocks fit together.

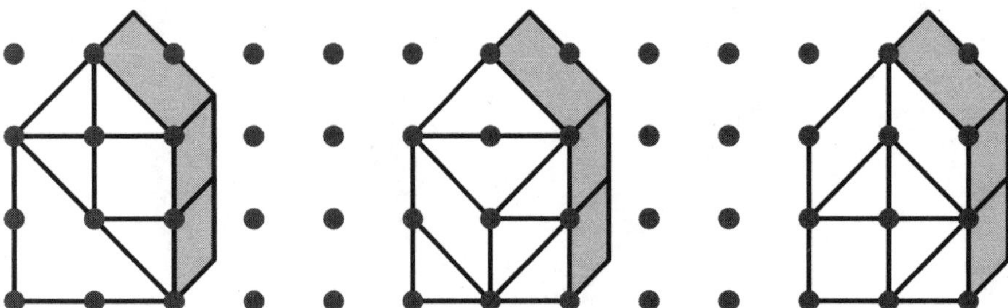

Draw in the lines to show other ways to fit the blocks together.

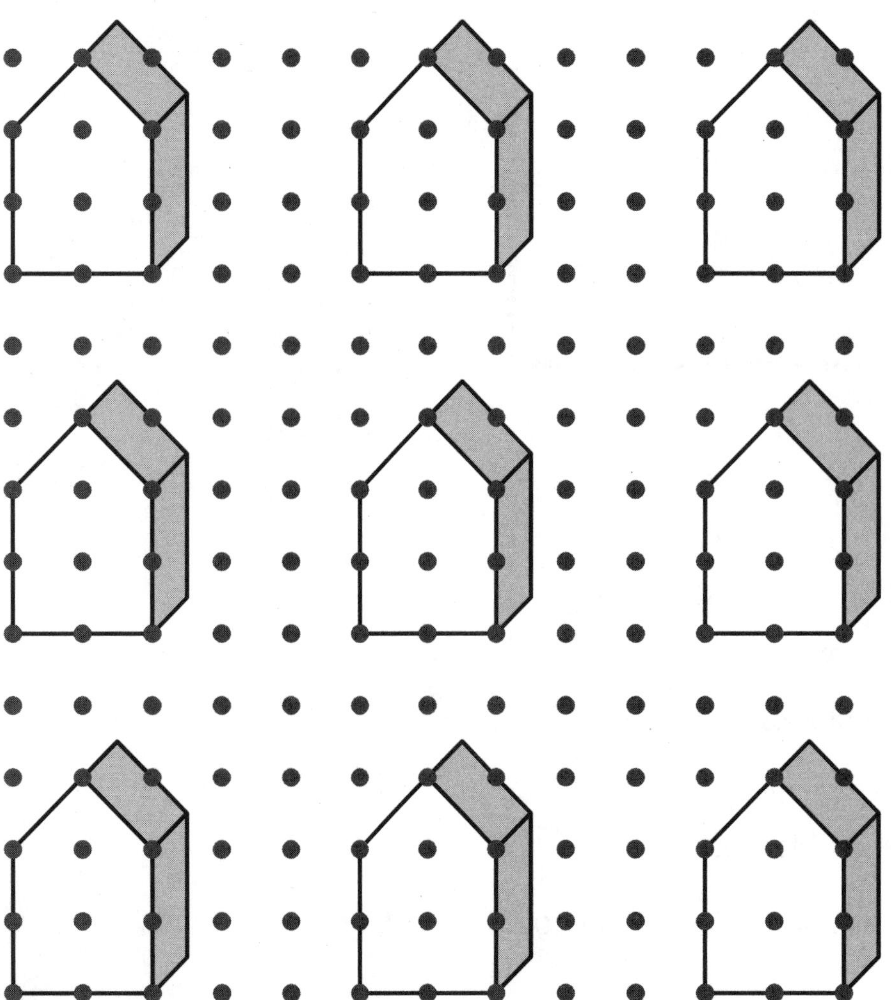

Hexagonal Prisms

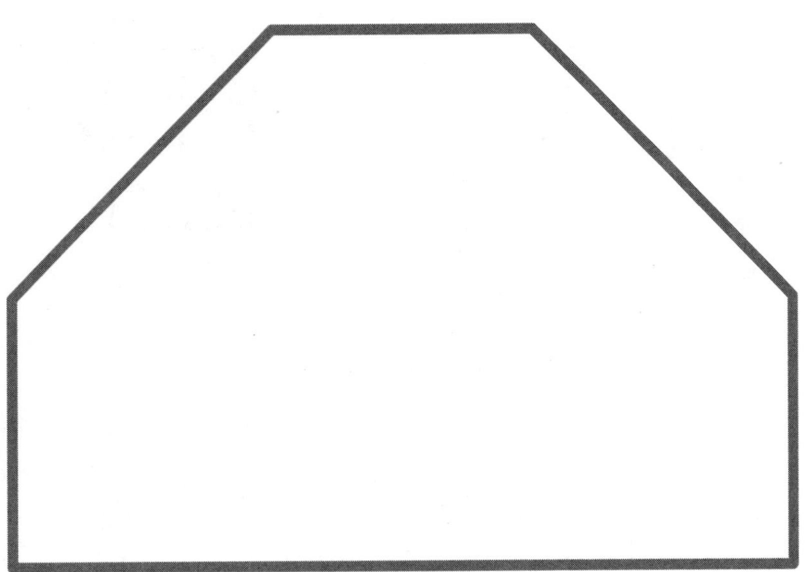

1. Fill the outline using
   a. five Tangram Blocks.
   b. six blocks.
   c. seven blocks.

2. Using different blocks, find another way to do a, b, and c.

Hexagonal Prisms

Here are pictures of how the Tangram Blocks fit together.

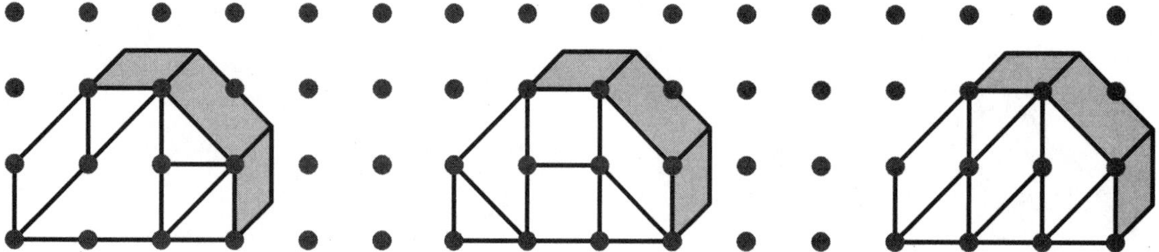

Draw in the lines to show other ways to fit the blocks together.

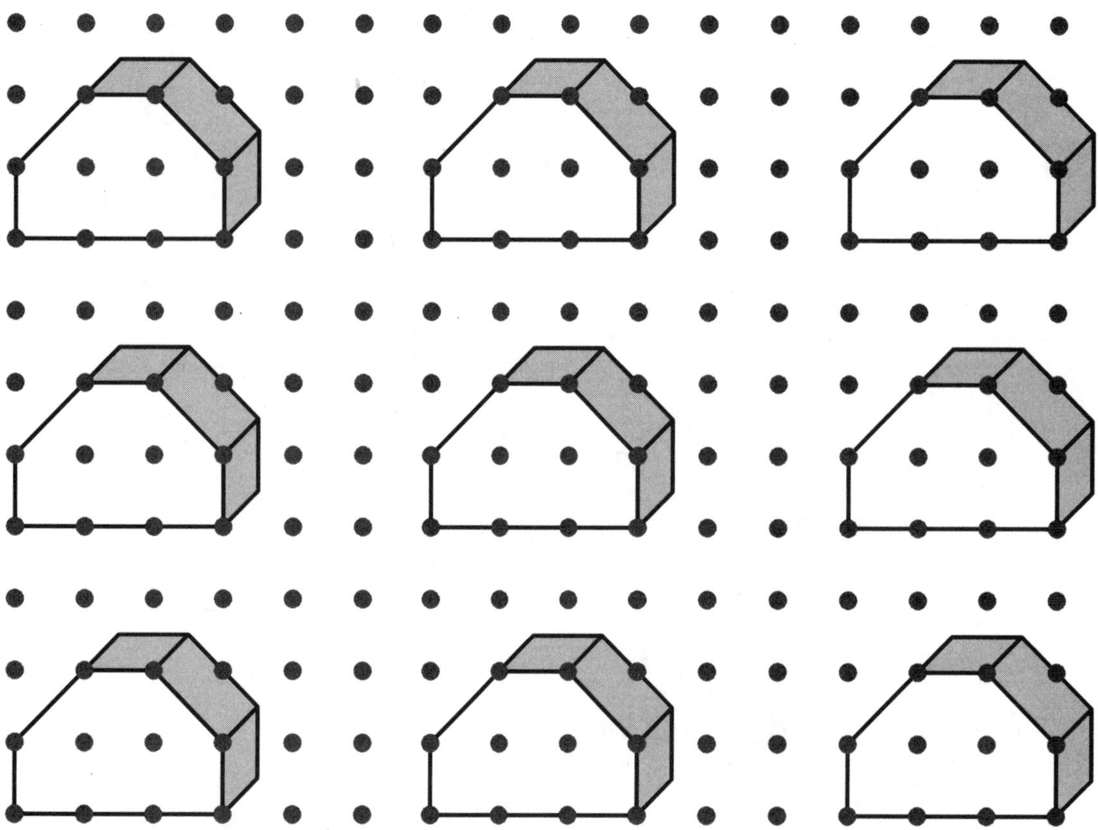

Answers can also be recorded on a copy of Appendix 2.

Rectangular Prisms

1. Fill the outline using
   a. four Tangram Blocks.
   b. five blocks.
   c. six blocks.
   d. seven blocks.
   e. eight blocks.

2. Using different blocks, find another way to do a, b, c, d, and e.

Rectangular Prisms

Here are pictures of how the Tangram Blocks fit together.

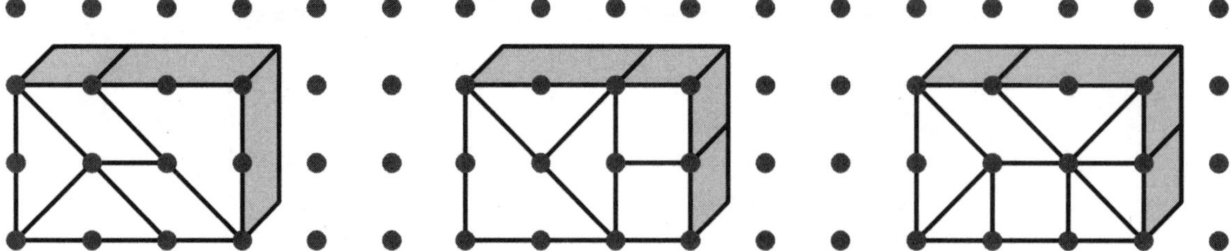

Draw in the lines to show other ways to fit the blocks together.

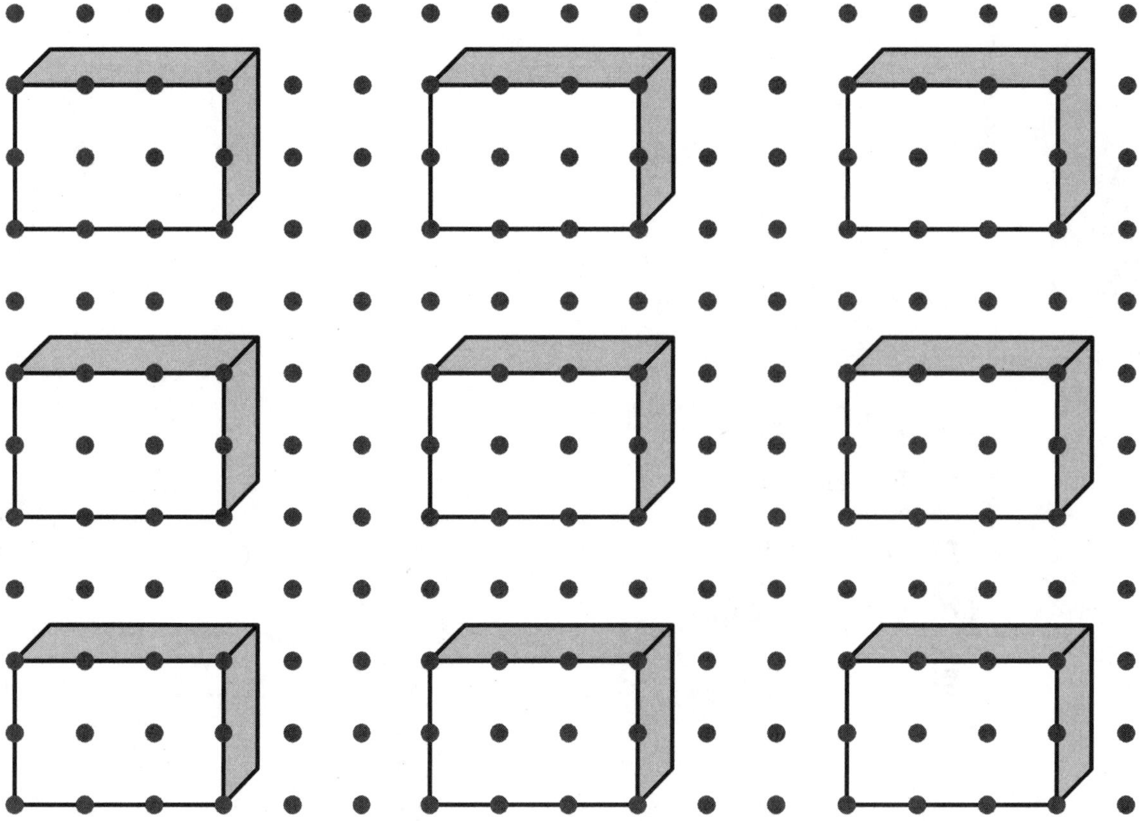

Numeral 0

1. Fill the outline with Tangram Blocks.

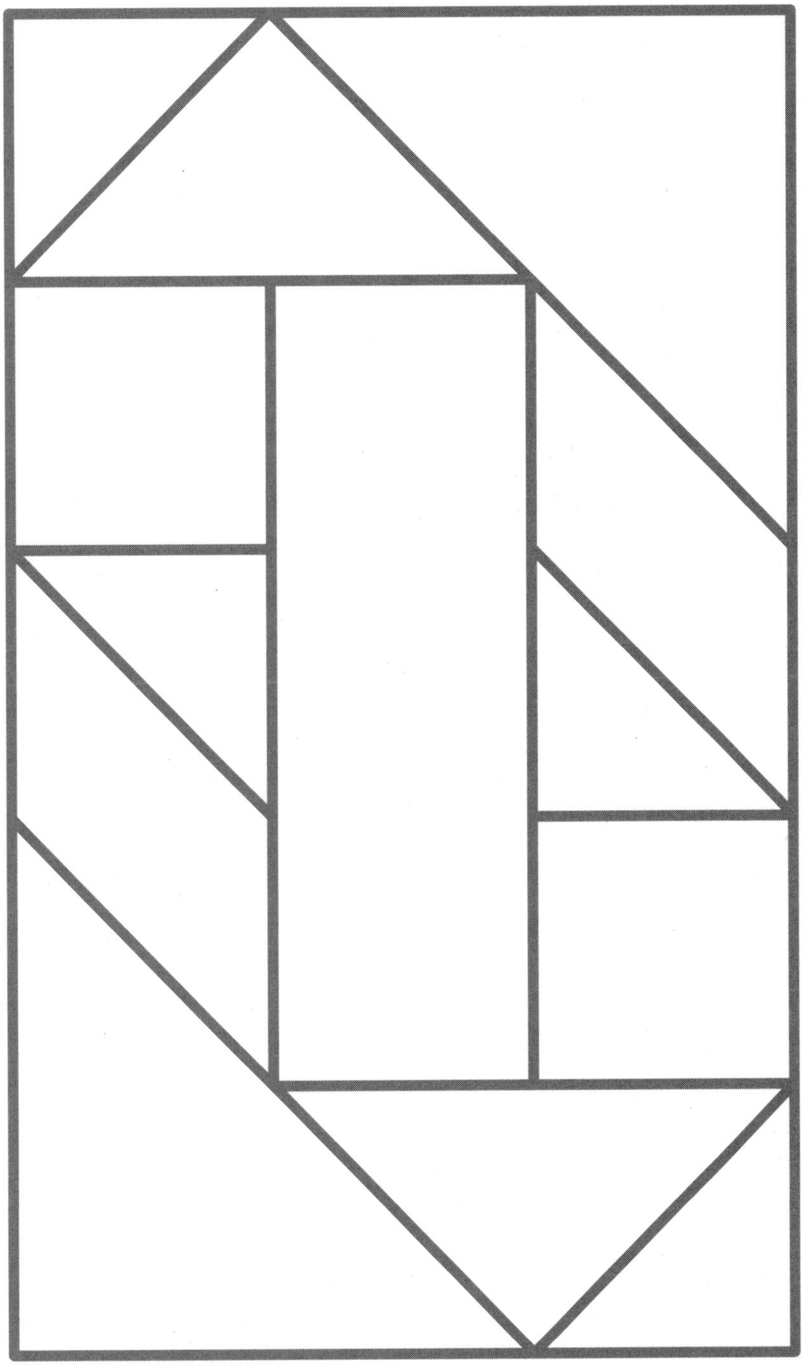

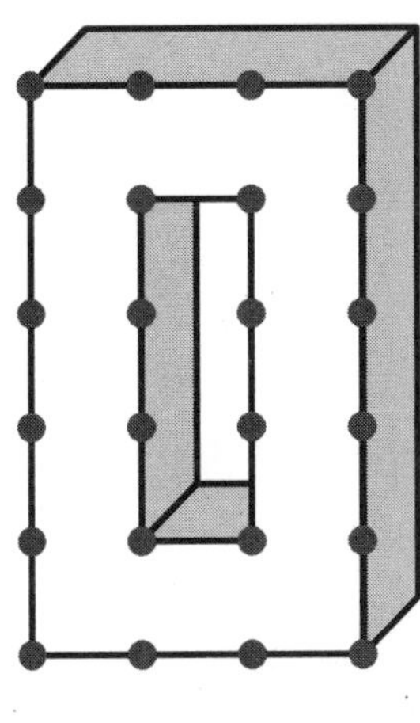

2. Draw on the small picture to show how the blocks fit together.

Numeral 1

1. Fill the outline with Tangram Blocks.

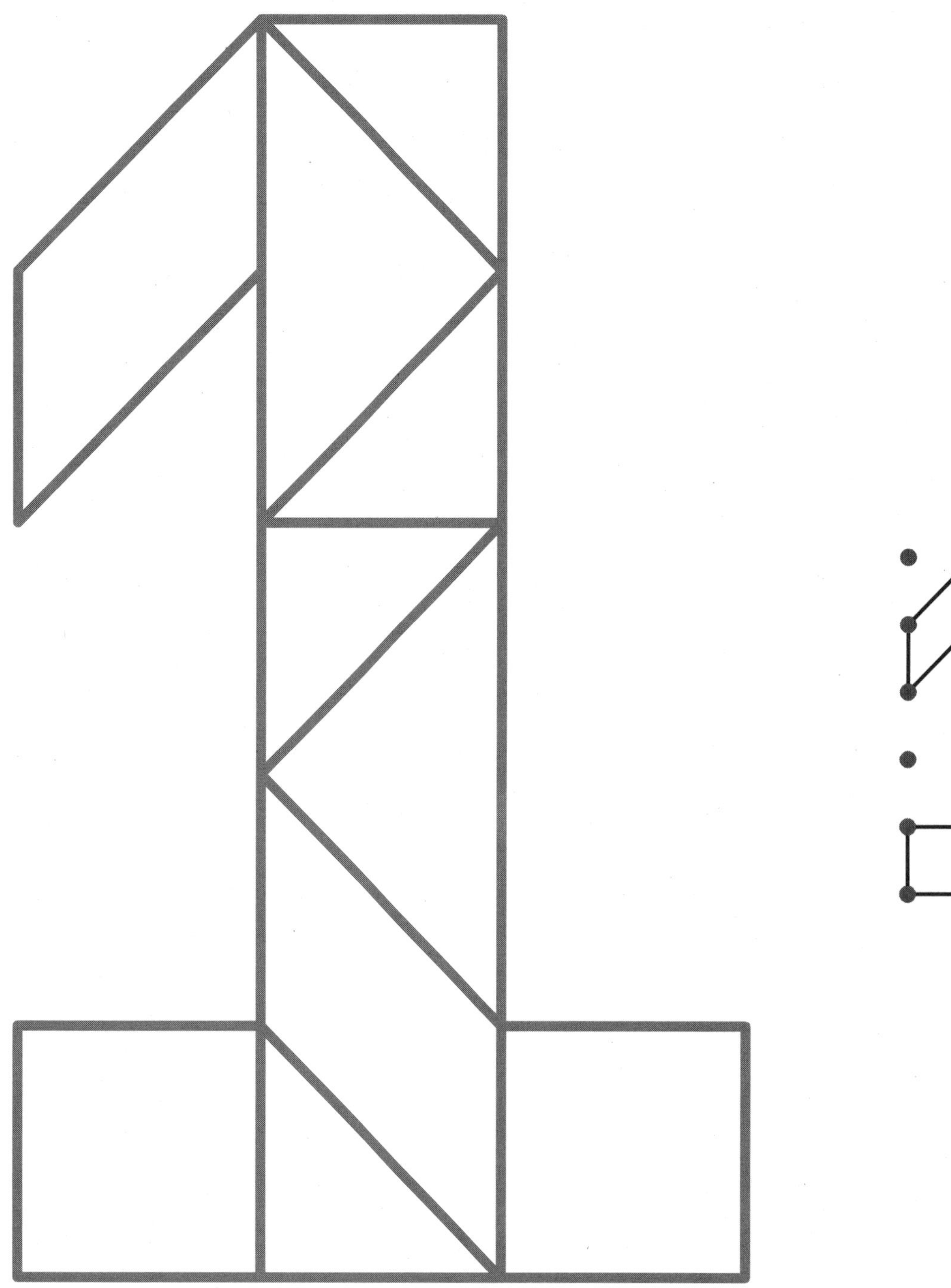

2. Draw on the small picture to show how the blocks fit together.

Numeral 2

1. Fill the outline with Tangram Blocks.

2. Draw on the small picture to show how the blocks fit together.

Numeral 3

1. Fill the outline with Tangram Blocks.

2. Draw on the small picture to show how the blocks fit together.

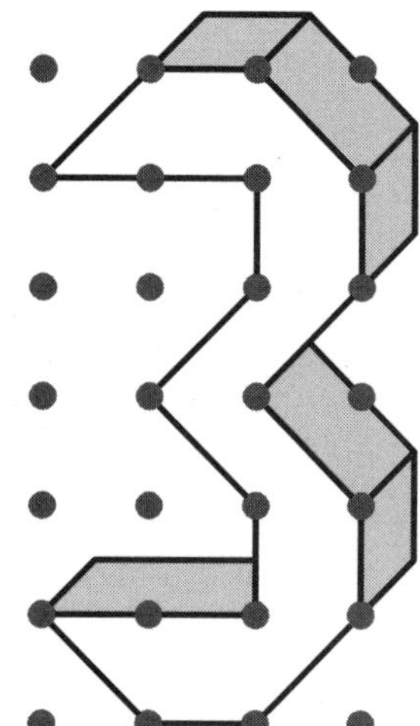

Numeral 4

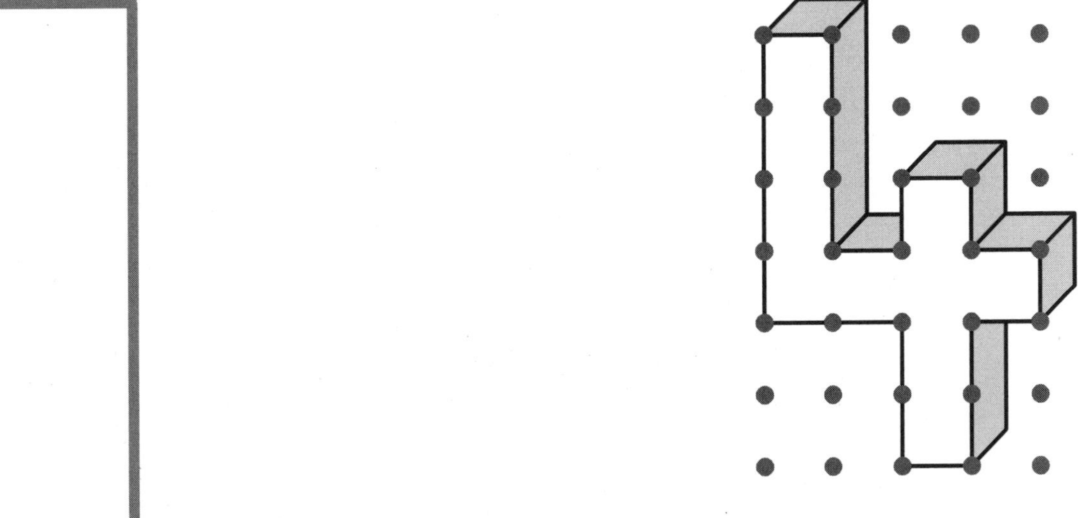

1. Fill the outline with Tangram Blocks.

2. Draw on the small picture to show how the blocks fit together.

Numeral 5

1. Fill the outline with Tangram Blocks.

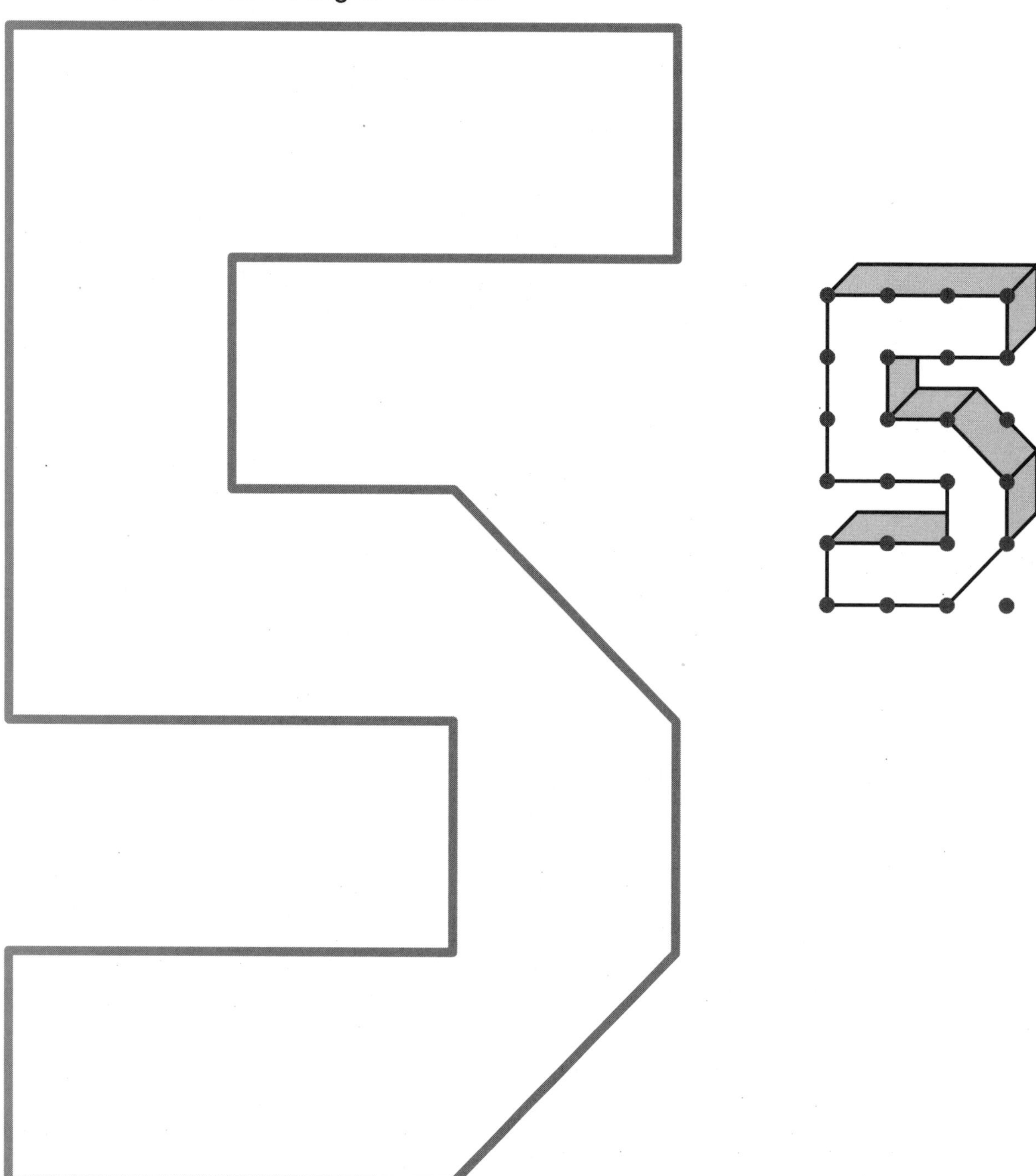

2. Draw on the small picture to show how the blocks fit together.

Numeral 6

1. Fill the outline with Tangram Blocks.

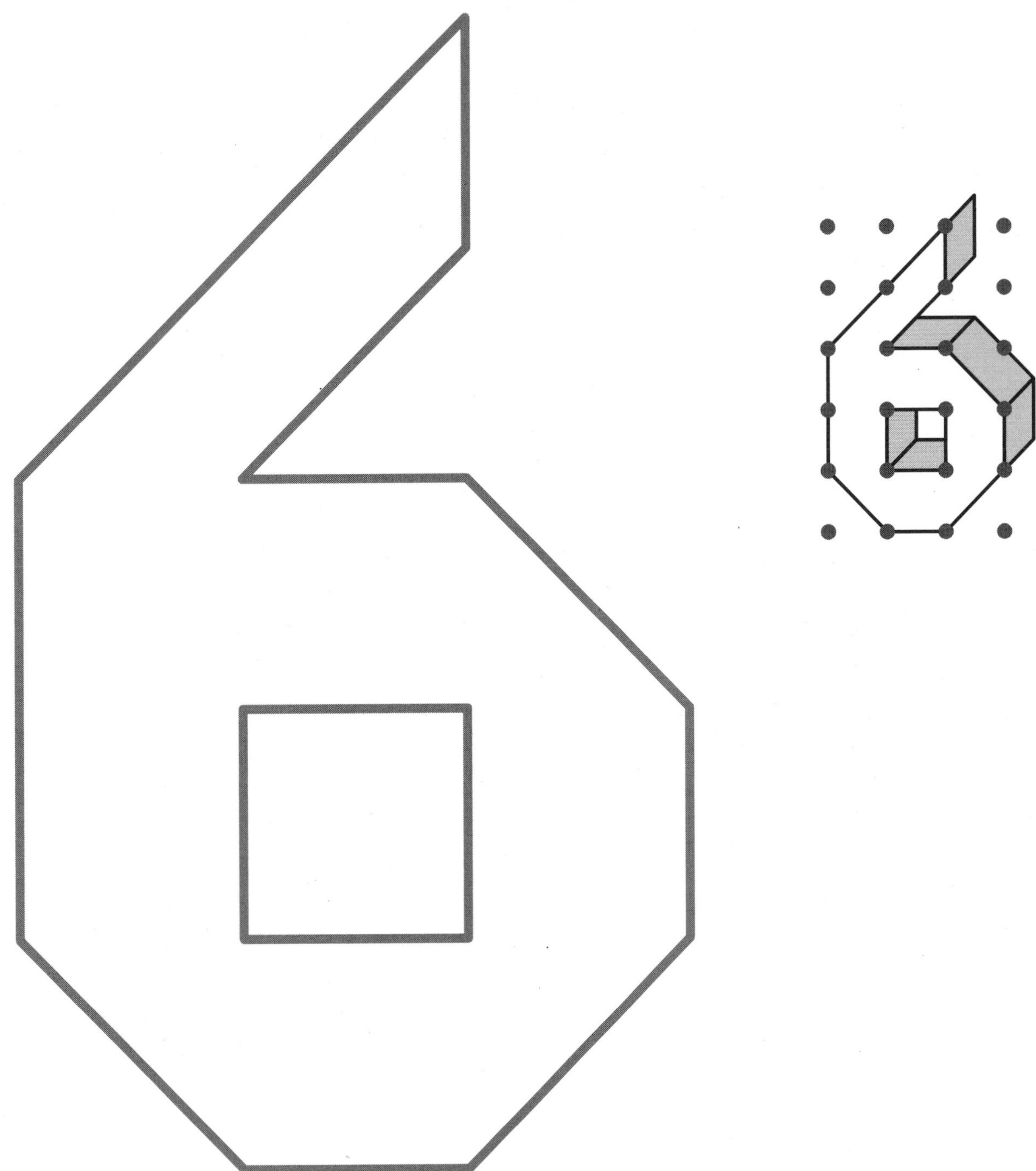

2. Draw on the small picture to show how the blocks fit together.

Numeral 7

1. Fill the outline with Tangram Blocks.

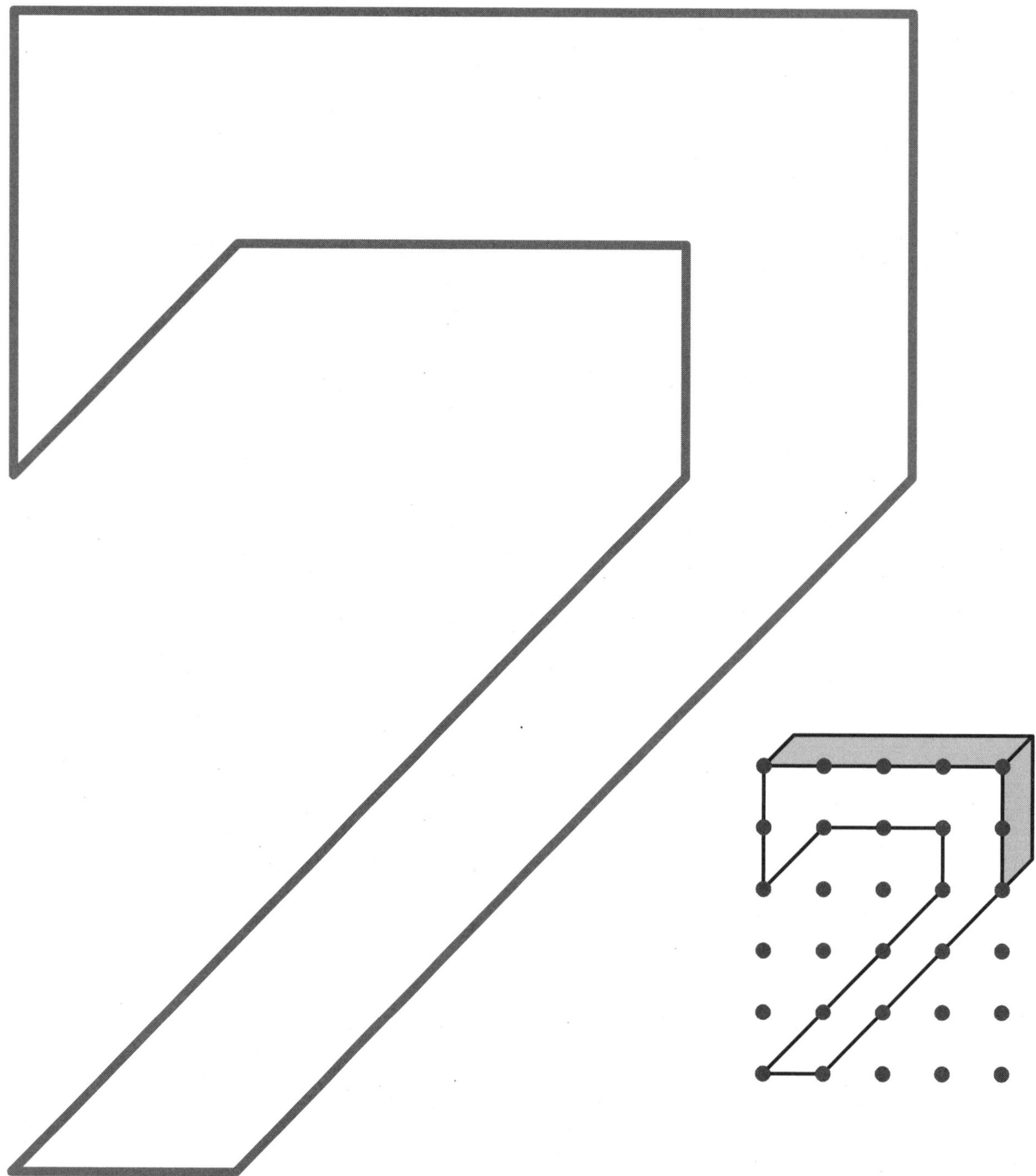

2. Draw on the small picture to show how the blocks fit together.

Numeral 8

1. Fill the outline with Tangram Blocks.

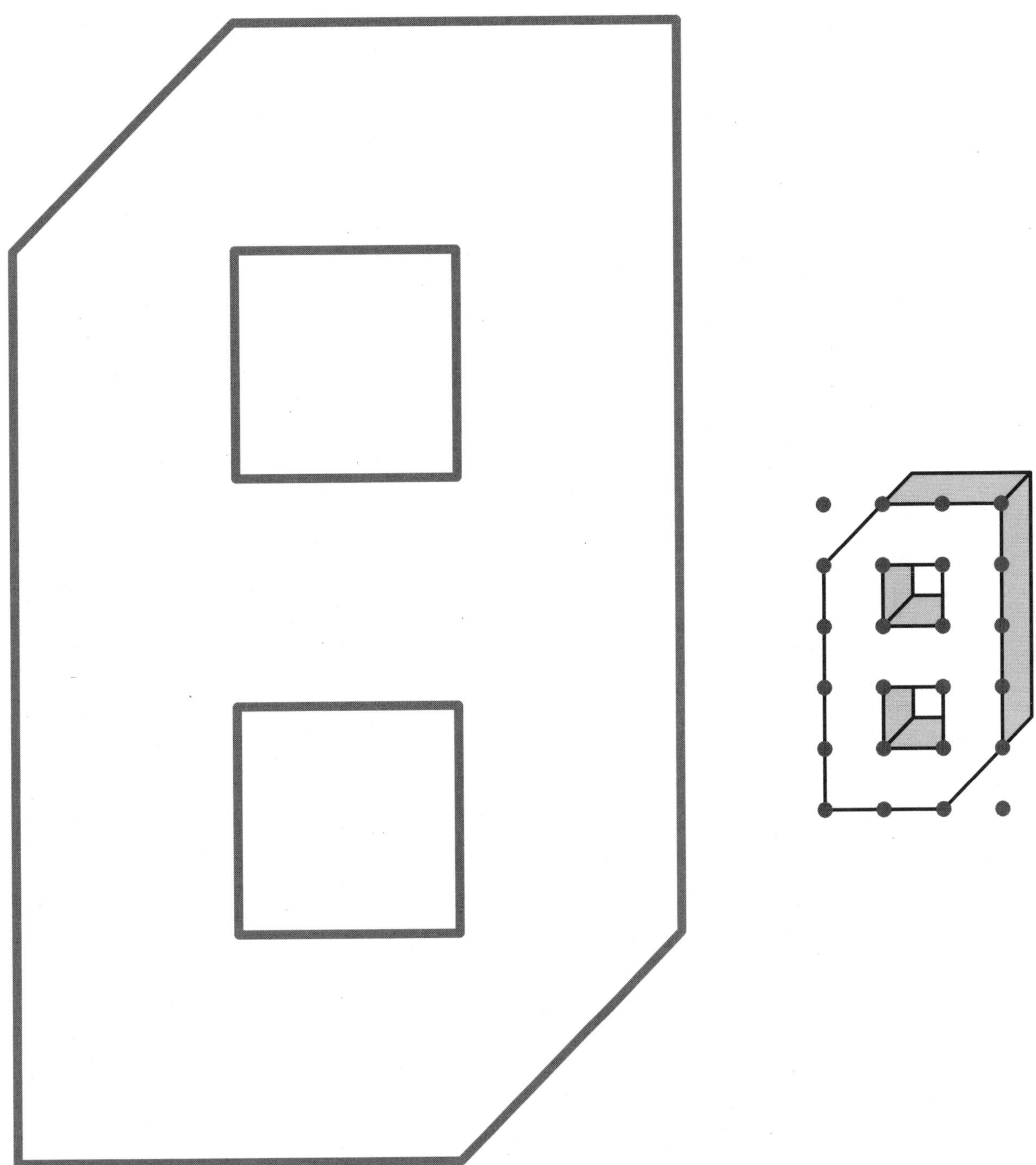

2. Draw on the small picture to show how the blocks fit together.

Numeral 9

1. Fill the outline with Tangram Blocks.

2. Draw on the small picture to show how the blocks fit together.

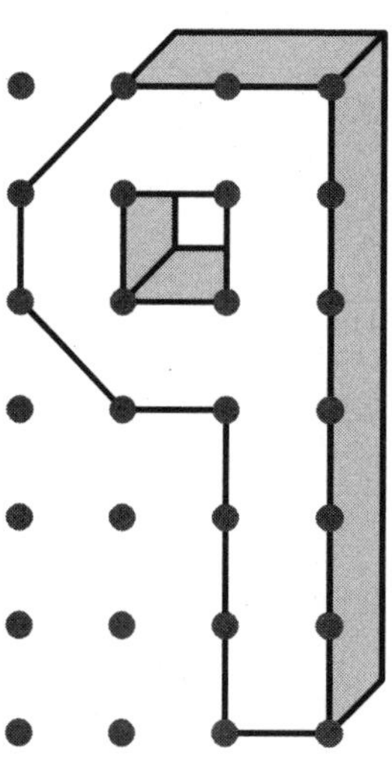

Chapter 3

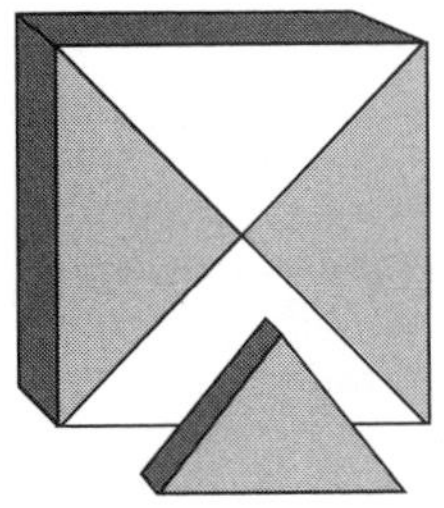

Block Buildings

Overview

Using the Tangram Blocks, students build prisms two or more levels high. This helps students develop an intuitive sense of volume. They continue to develop spatial skills by using two-dimensional drawings to represent three-dimensional objects. They record solutions by levels. Descriptive vocabulary is used to label the prisms. Activities include building and recording selected types of the following prisms:

- triangular
- parallelepiped
- rectangular
- trapezoidal

You may notice the following while observing students working on this section.

- Students enjoy the "bigness" of the appropriate vocabulary.
- In completing the activities, students develop strategies for matching the blocks together to build the assigned figures.

Note: The answers to Activities 3–12 can be recorded on Appendix 2. The answers to Activities 13–16 can be recorded on Appendix 3.

Triangular Prisms

Use these Tangram Blocks: four small triangular prisms.

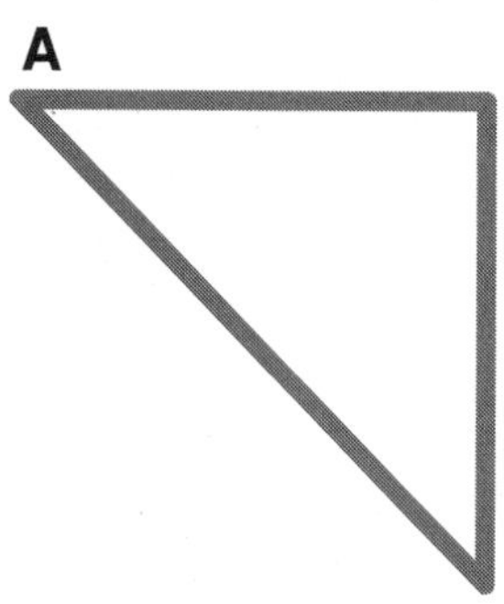

1. Build a tall triangular prism by stacking the blocks on outline A. Match the triangular faces.

2. Put the blocks on outline B. Match the triangular faces.

3. Put the blocks on outline C. Match the triangular faces.

4. How are the buildings in A, B, and C the same? ______________________

____

Triangular Prisms

A

Use these Tangram Blocks: four small triangular prisms and two medium triangular prisms.

1. Stack the blocks on outline A to build a tall triangular prism.

2. Put the blocks on outline B to build a triangular prism.

B

3. Put the blocks on outline C to build a triangular prism.

C

4. How are the triangular prisms in A, B, and C the same? ____________________

____

Triangular Prisms

Use these Tangram Blocks: 12 of the 14 blocks.

1. Stack the blocks on the outline to build a triangular prism that is seven levels high.

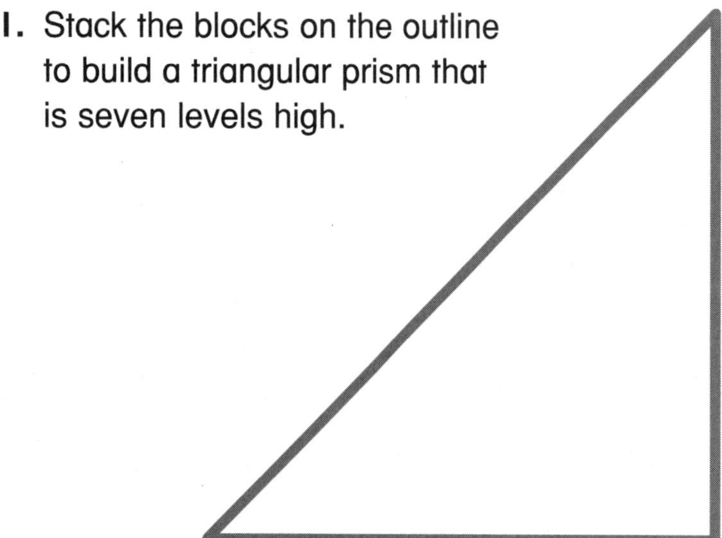

2. Draw on the pictures below to show each level. Start with level one, which is the bottom level.

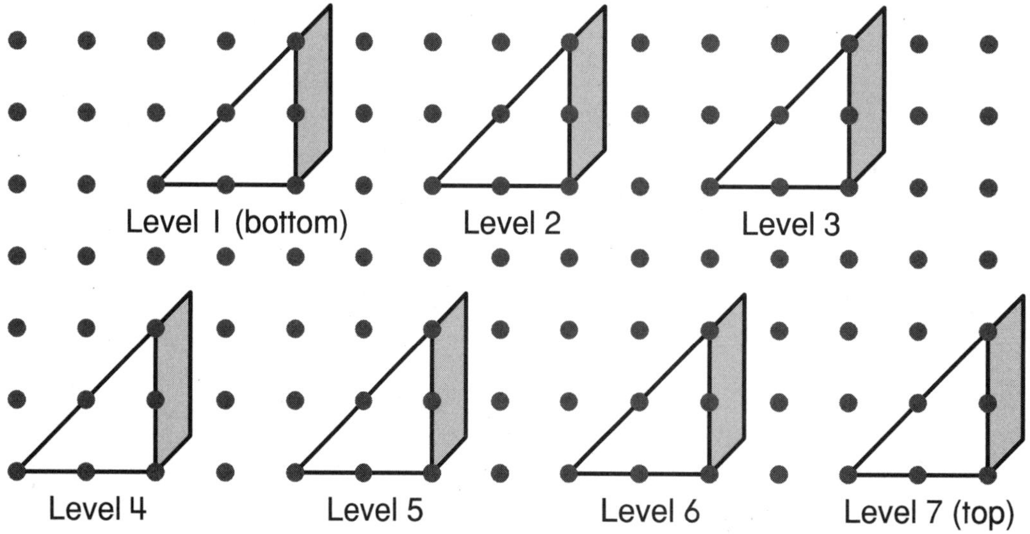

Triangular Prisms

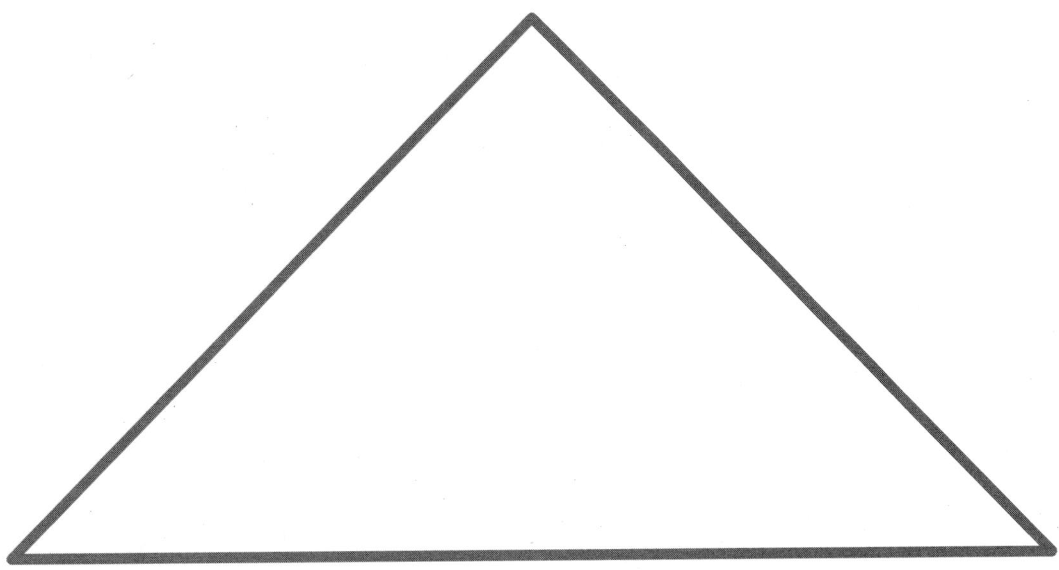

Use these Tangram Blocks: ten triangular prisms.

1. Stack the blocks on the outline to build a triangular prism that is three levels high.

2. Draw on the pictures below to show each level. Start with level one, the bottom level.

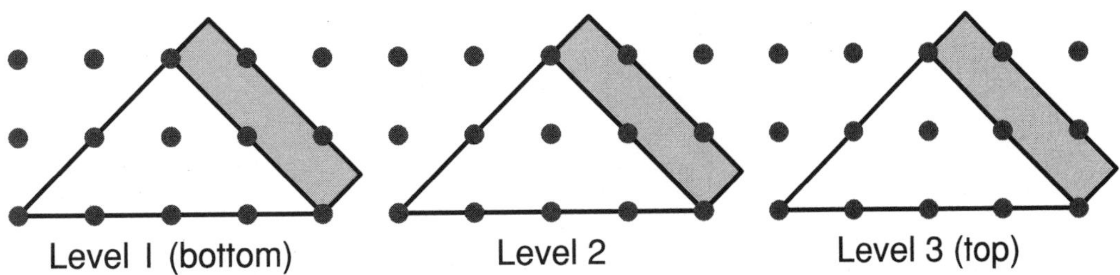

Triangular Prisms

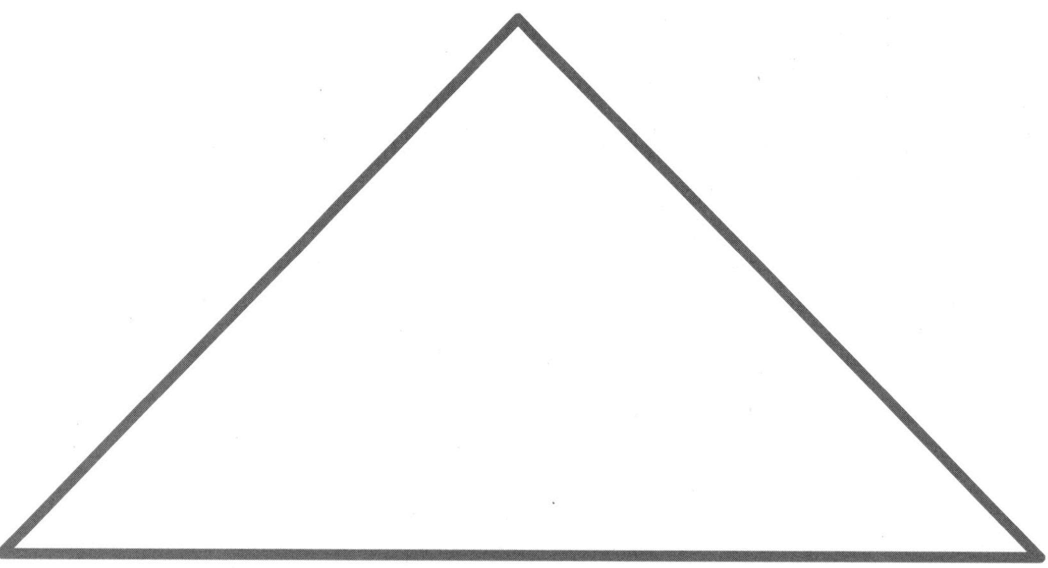

Use these Tangram Blocks: eight triangular prisms, one cube, and one parallelepiped.

1. Stack the blocks on the outline to build a triangular prism that is three levels high.

2. Draw on the pictures below to show each level. Start with level one, the bottom level.

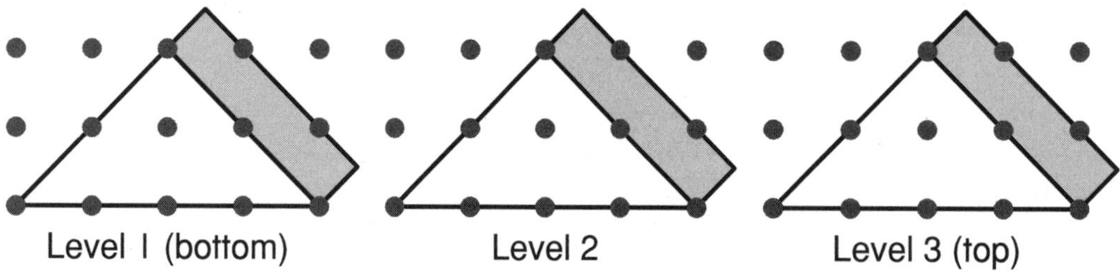

Triangular Prisms

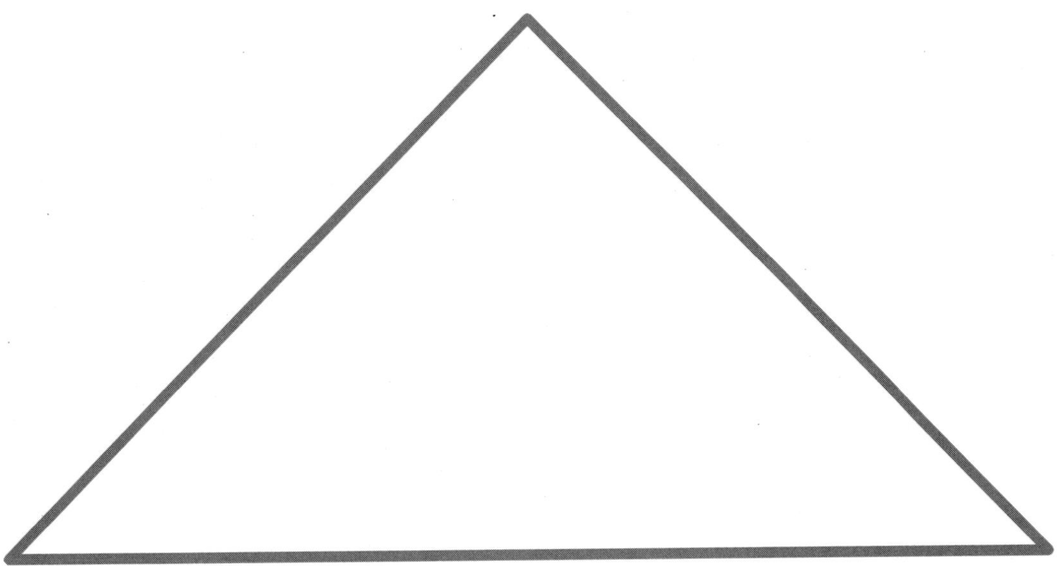

Use all 14 Tangram Blocks.

1. Stack the blocks on the outline to build a triangular prism that is four levels high.

2. Draw on the pictures below to show each level. Start with level one, the bottom level.

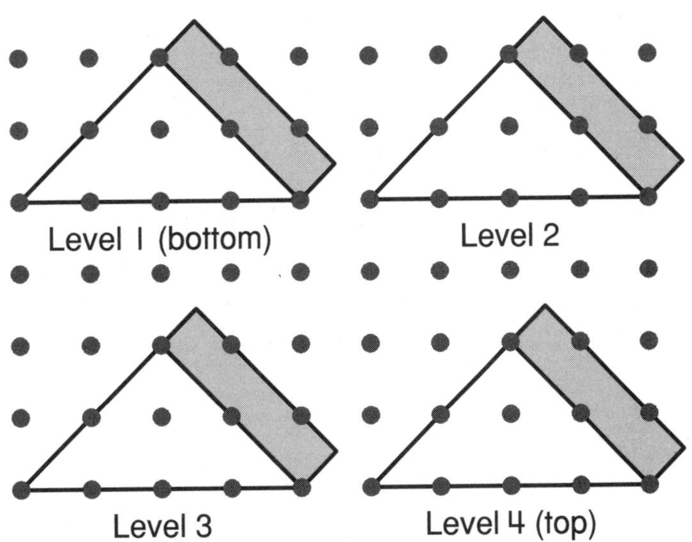

Parallelepipeds

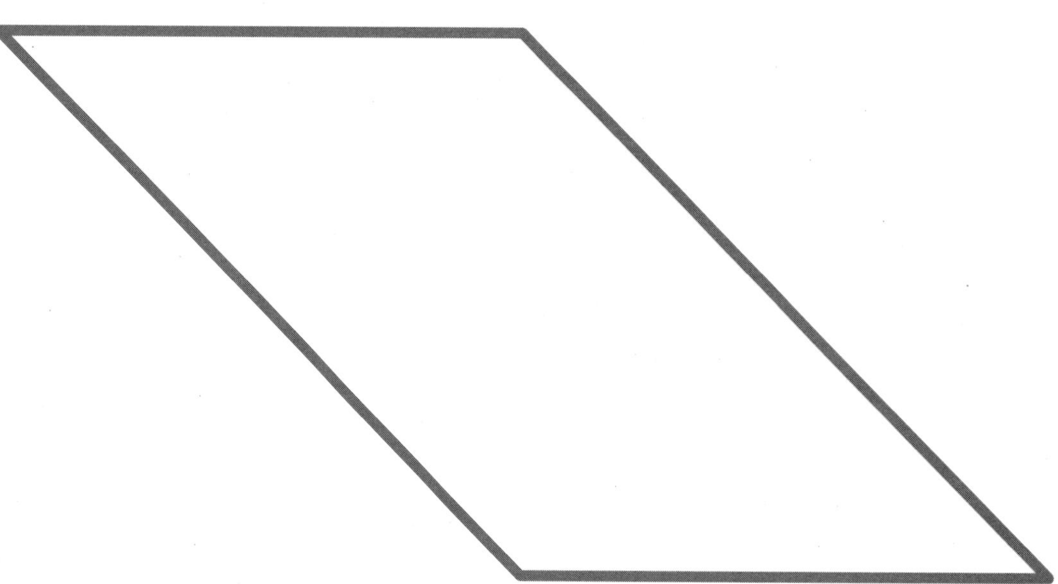

Use these Tangram Blocks: ten triangular prisms.

1. Stack the blocks on the outline to build a parallelepiped that is three levels high.

2. Draw on the pictures below to show each level. Start with level one, the bottom level.

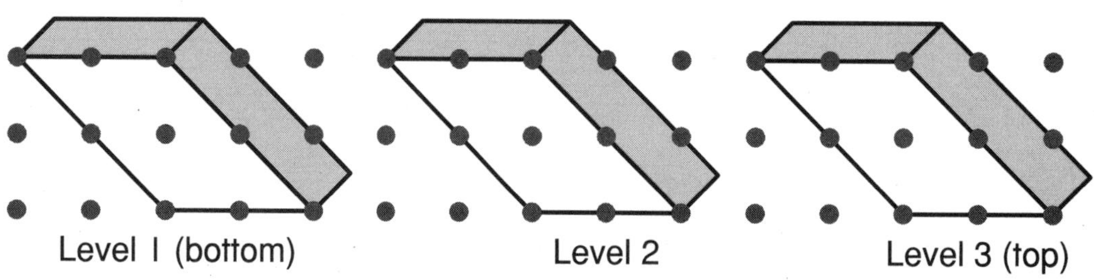

Parallelepipeds

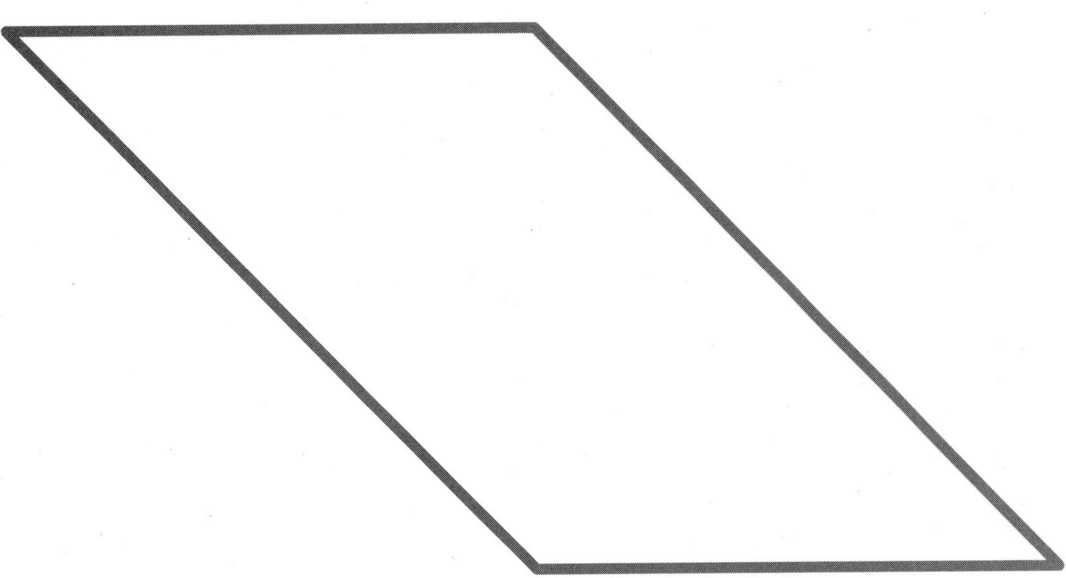

Use these Tangram Blocks: nine triangular prisms, one cube, and one parallelepiped.

1. Stack the blocks on the outline to build a parallelepiped that is three levels high.

2. Draw on the pictures below to show each level. Start with level one, the bottom level.

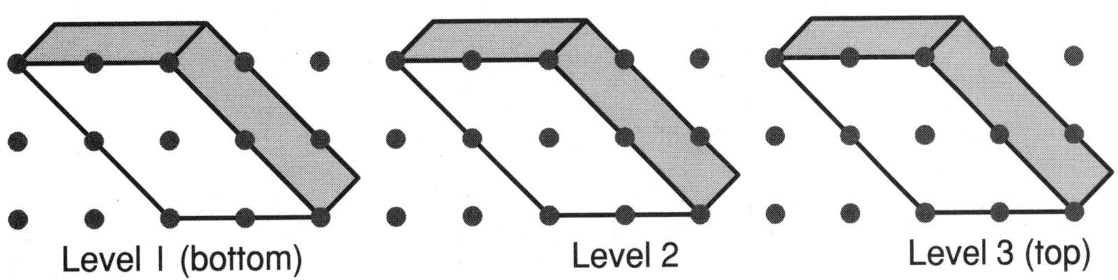

Parallelepipeds

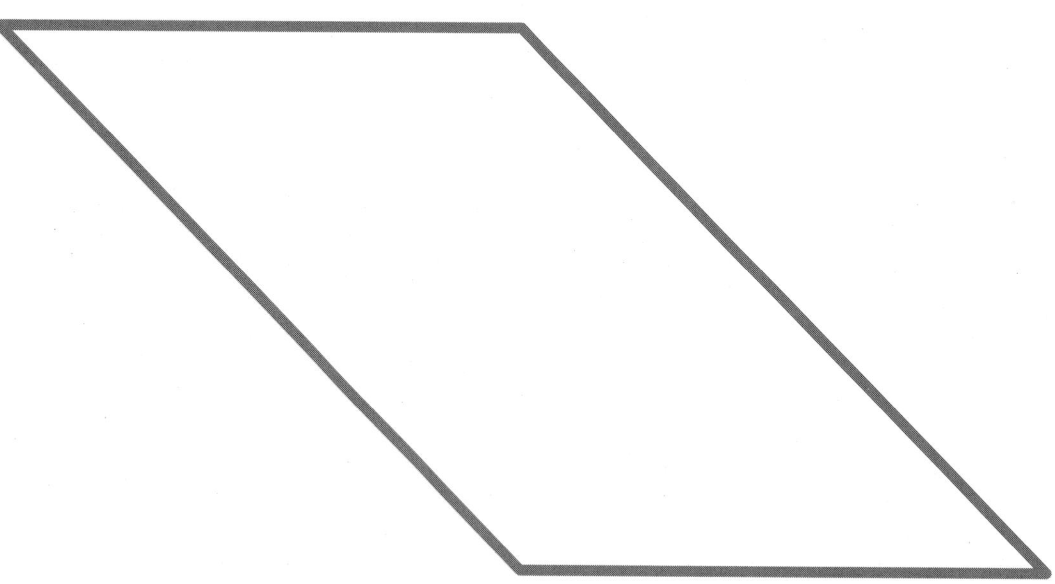

Use all 14 Tangram Blocks.

1. Stack the blocks on the outline to build a parallelepiped that is four levels high.

2. Draw on the pictures below to show each level. Start with level one, the bottom level.

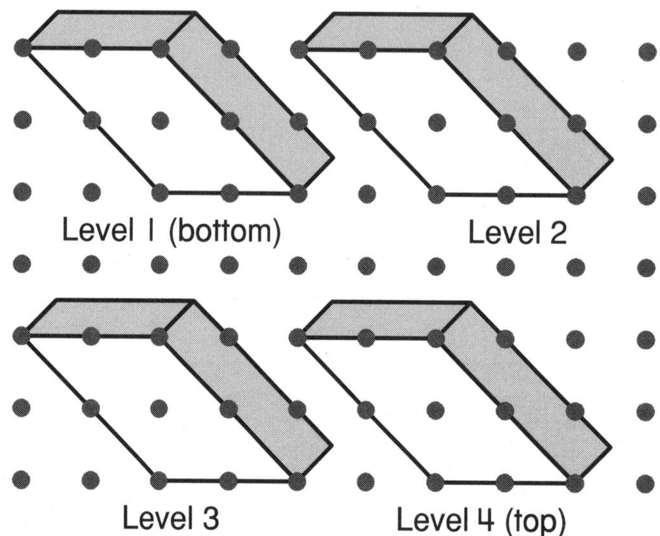

Rectangular Prisms

Use these Tangram Blocks: ten triangular prisms.

1. Stack the blocks on the outline to build a large rectangular prism that is three levels high.

2. Draw on the pictures below to show each level. Start with level one, the bottom level.

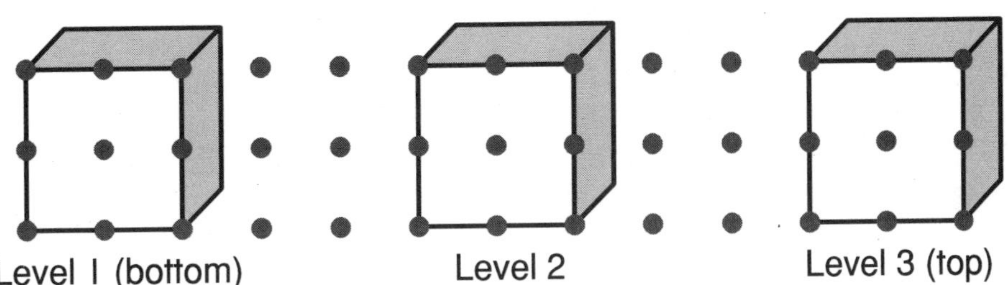

Rectangular Prisms

Use these Tangram Blocks: seven triangular prisms, two cubes, and one parallelepiped.

1. Stack the blocks on the outline to build a large rectangular prism that is three levels high.

2. Draw on the pictures below to show each level. Start with level one, the bottom level.

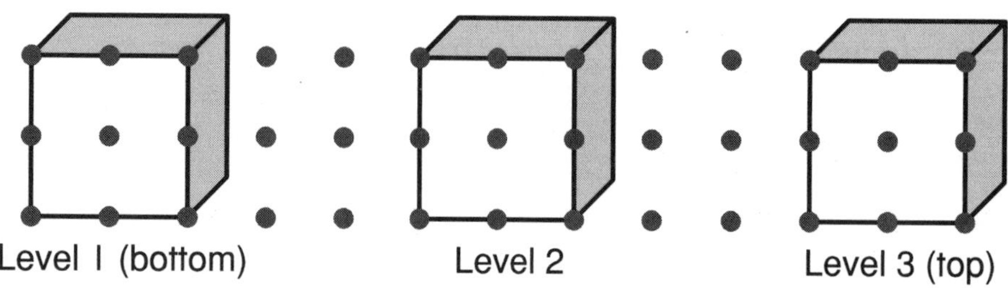

Rectangular Prisms

Use all 14 Tangram Blocks.

1. Stack the blocks on the outline to build a large rectangular prism that is four levels high.

2. Draw on the pictures below to show each level. Start with level one, the bottom level.

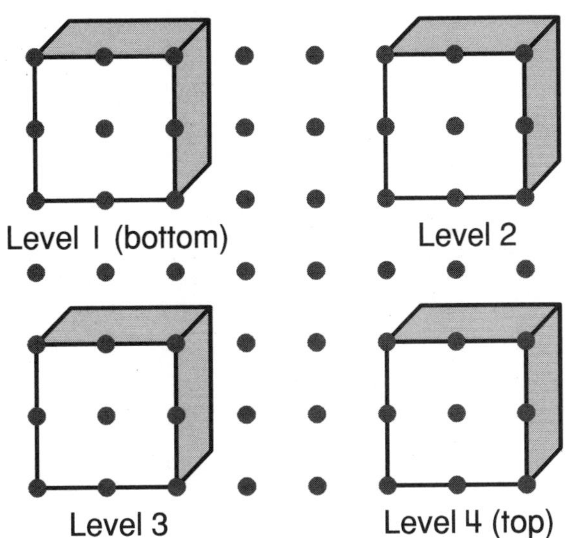

Trapezoidal Prisms

Use all 14 Tangram Blocks.

1. Stack the blocks on the outline to build a large trapezoidal prism that is two levels high.

2. Draw on the pictures below to show each level. Start with level one, the bottom level.

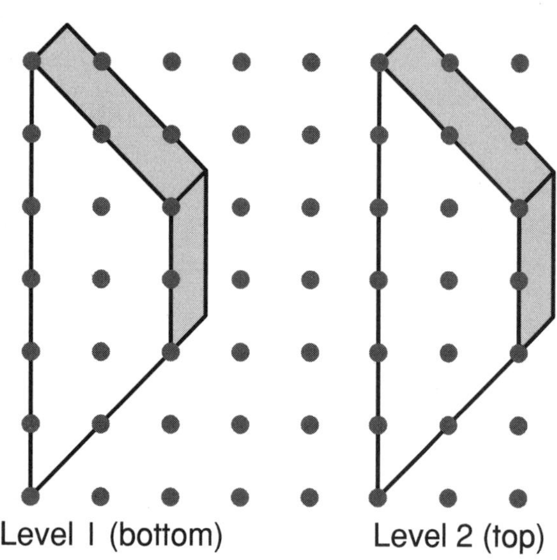

Trapezoidal Prisms

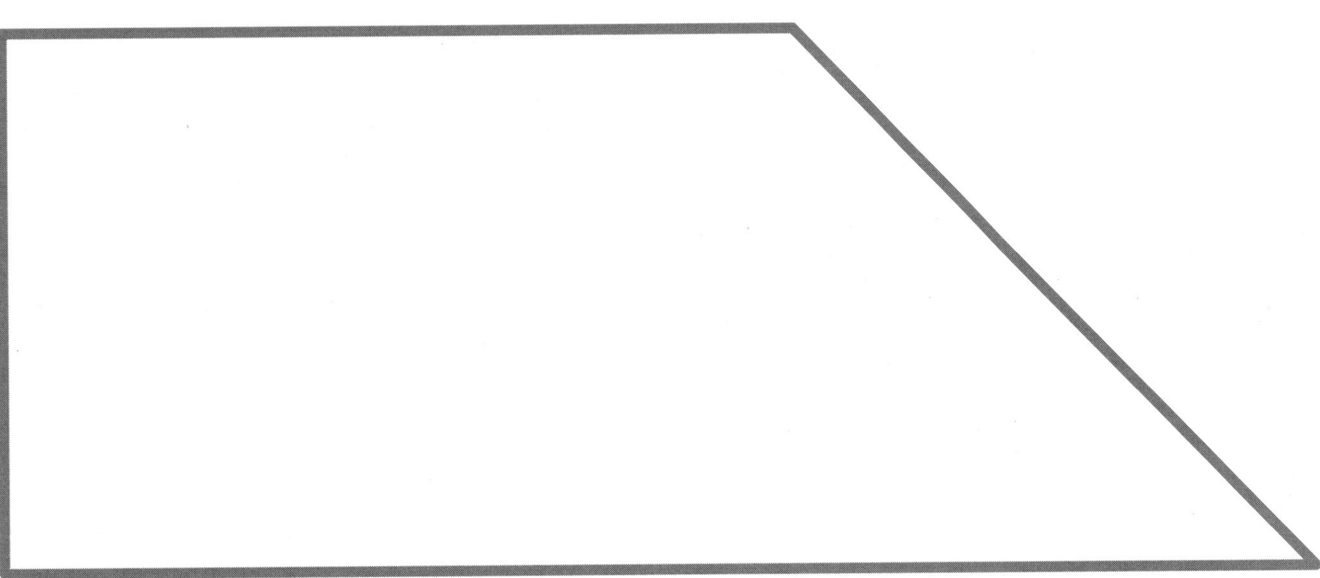

Use all 14 Tangram Blocks.

1. Stack the blocks on the outline to build a large trapezoidal prism that is two levels high.

2. Draw on the pictures below to show each level. Start with level one, the bottom level.

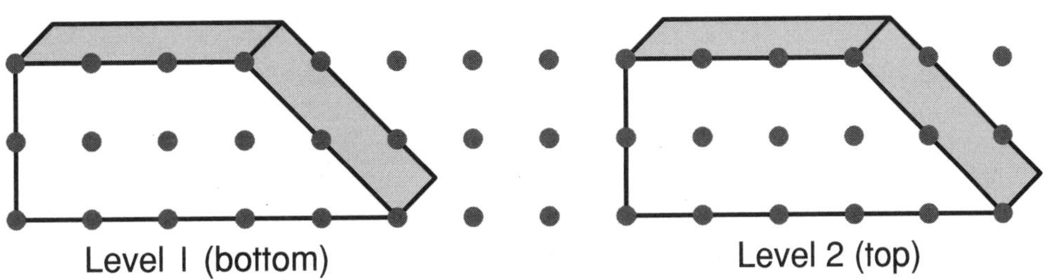

Level 1 (bottom) Level 2 (top)

Trapezoidal Prisms

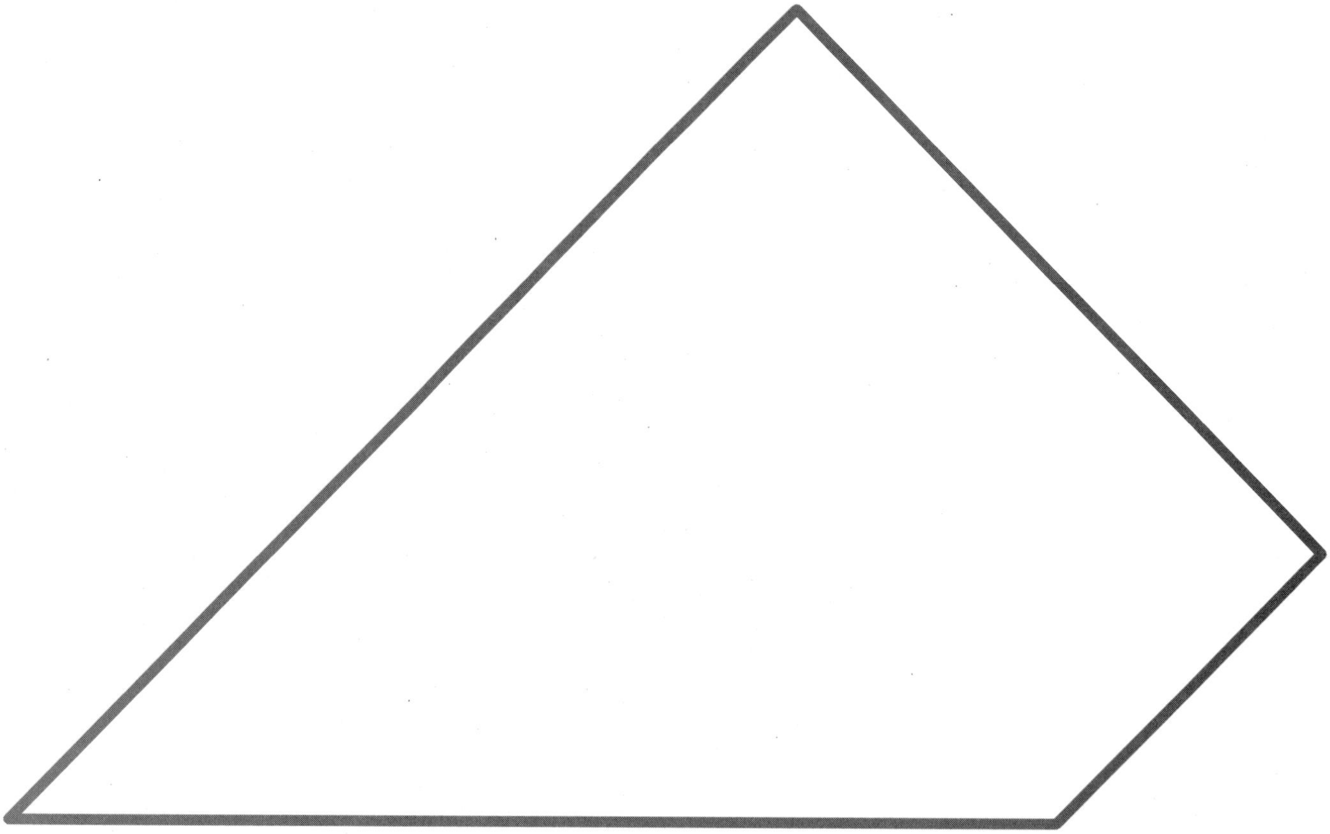

Use all 14 Tangram Blocks.

1. Stack the blocks on the outline to build a large trapezoidal prism that is two levels high.

2. Draw on the pictures below to show each level. Start with level one, the bottom level.

Level 1 (bottom)

Level 2 (top)

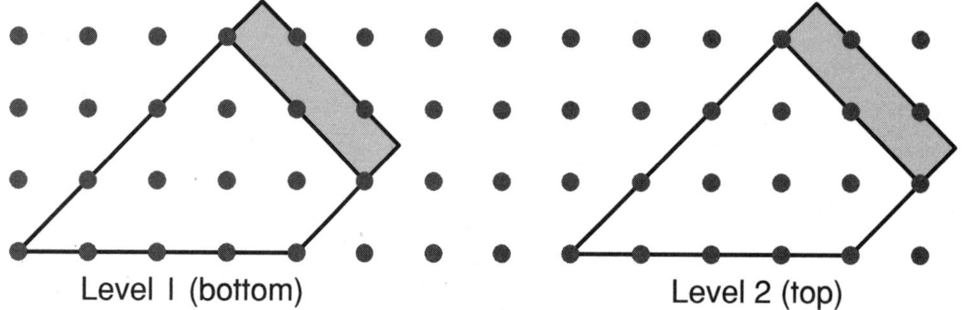

Trapezoidal Prisms

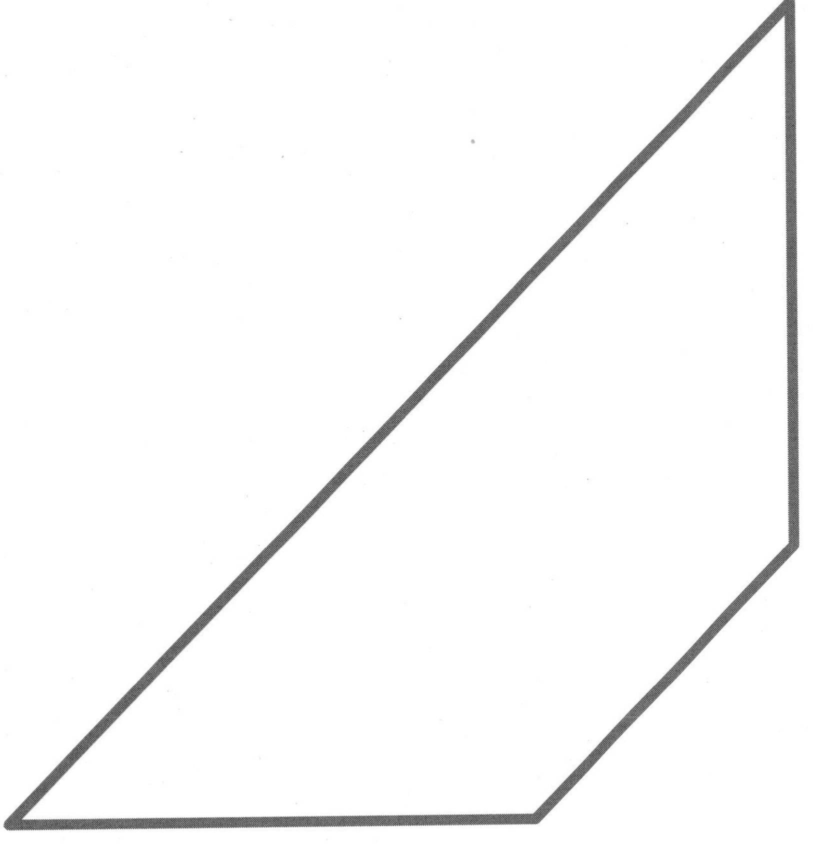

Use all 14 Tangram Blocks.

1. Stack the blocks on the outline to build a large trapezoidal prism that is four levels high.

2. Draw on the pictures below to show each level. Start with level one, the bottom level.

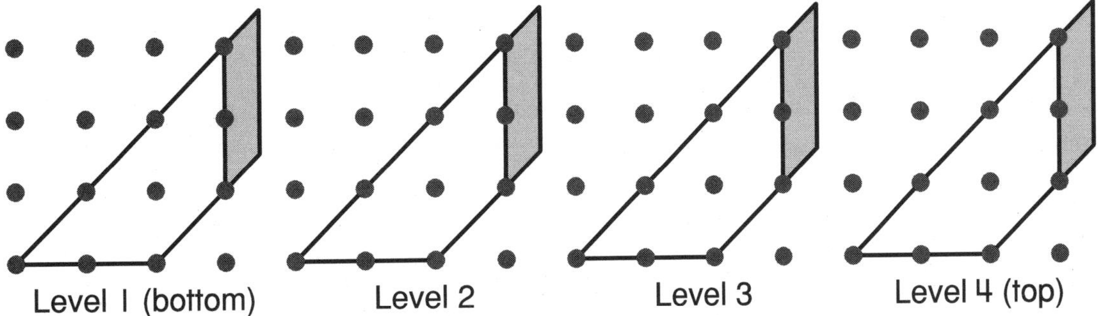

Chapter 4

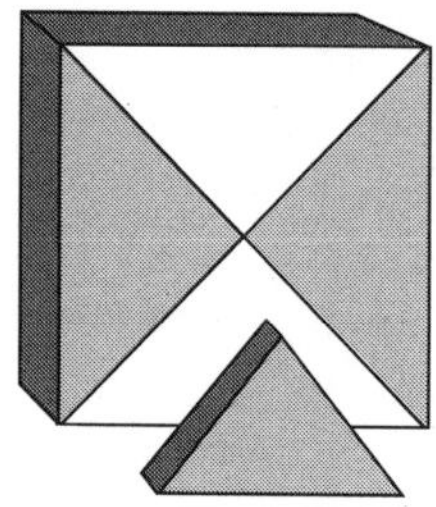

Symmetry Patterns

Overview

In this section, students develop their perception of spatial relationships by looking at a group of Tangram Blocks from the viewpoint of symmetry patterns. Specifically, they view a group of blocks in relation to a second, congruent set of blocks, that together form one larger symmetric figure. Students do the following:

- Place congruent blocks together on opposite sides of a line of symmetry.
- Build symmetric figures using various groups of blocks and a specified line of symmetry.
- Record solutions on dot paper and indicate lines of symmetry.
- Learn vocabulary including heptagonal and octagonal prisms.

You may notice the following while observing students working on this section.

- Students enjoy creating symmetric patterns.
- They appreciate and easily understand the impact of color in symmetric designs.
- Students want to use colored pencils to color in their designs rather than simply labeling them with appropriate descriptive names.

Note: The answers to Activities 2–16 can be recorded on Appendix 3.

Lines of Symmetry

A line of symmetry divides a shape into two parts. Each part is the mirror image of the other.

1. Place two Tangram Block cubes side by side. The tops of the two blocks form a shape. Find a line of symmetry that divides the shape into two symmetric parts.

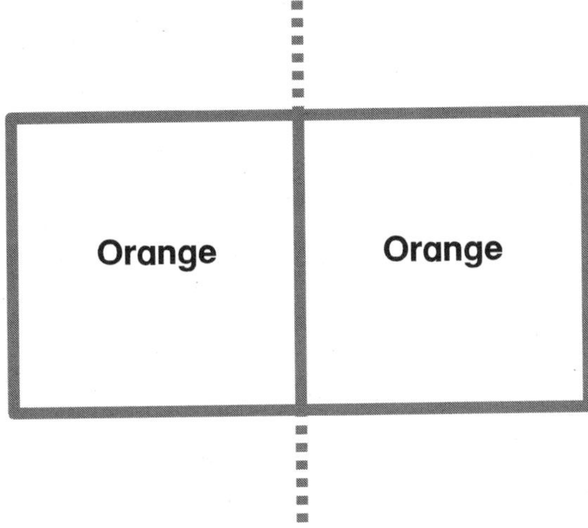

2. Place two small triangular prisms side by side. Find a line of symmetry that divides the shape into two symmetric parts. Try to arrange the blocks in a different way and find a new line of symmetry.

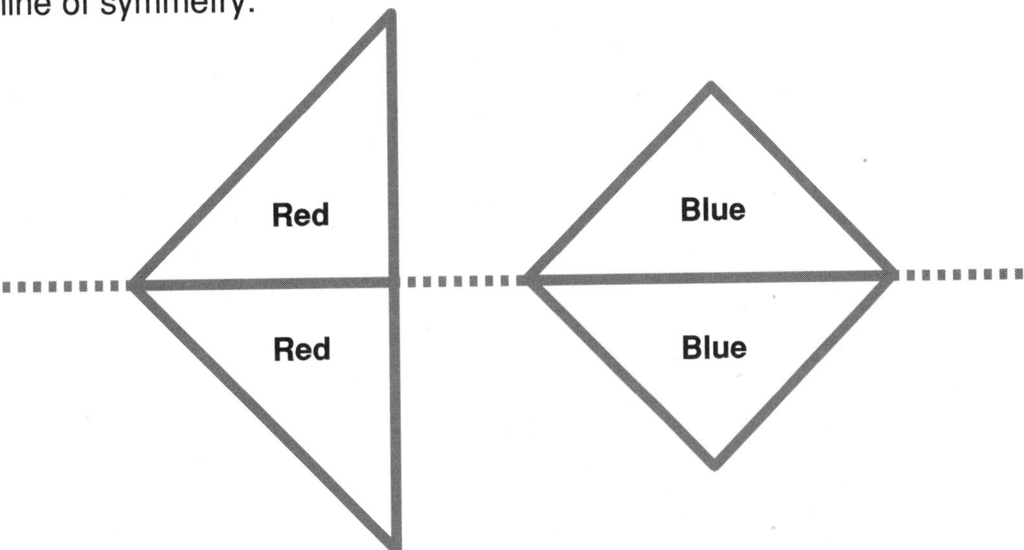

Lines of Symmetry

1. Place three Tangram Blocks as shown.

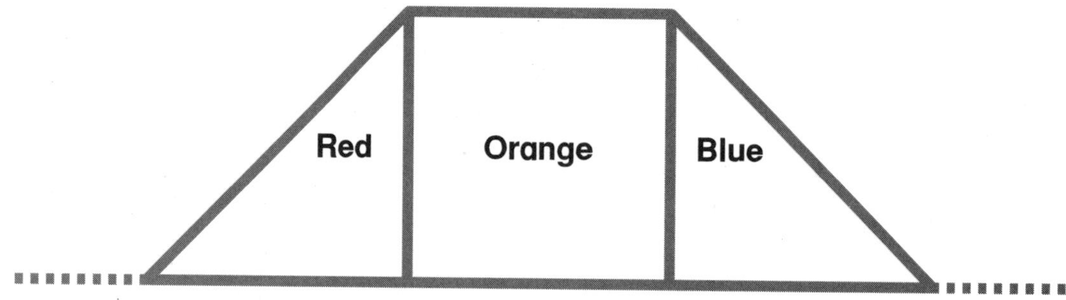

2. Place blocks below the above shape to make the dotted line a line of symmetry.

3. The completed figure is called a *hexagonal* prism. Draw the blocks on the picture below. Label *R* for red blocks and *B* for blue blocks.

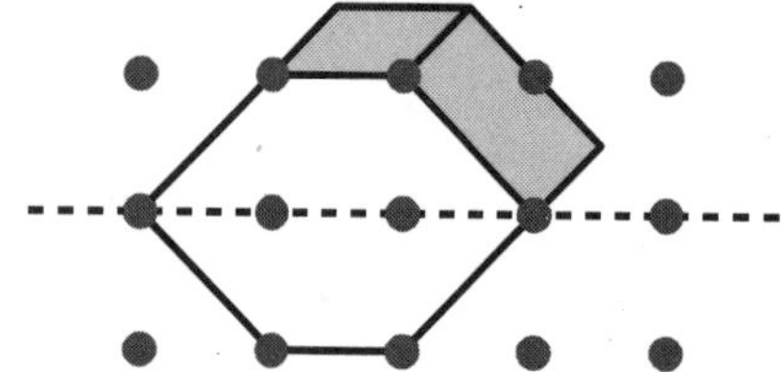

Lines of Symmetry

1. Place two Tangram Blocks as shown.

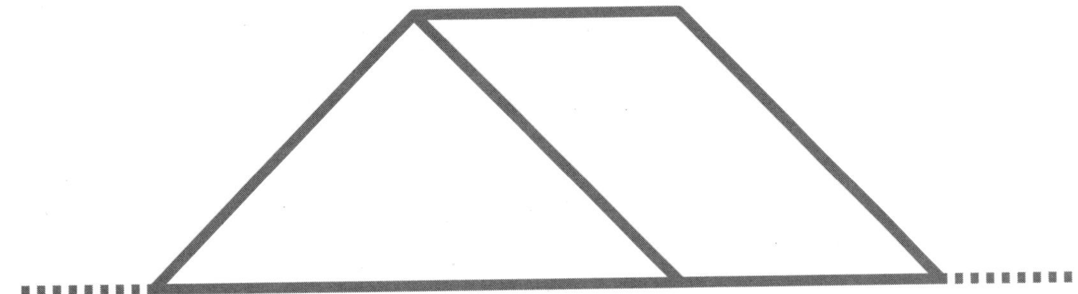

2. Place blocks below the above shape to make the dotted line a line of symmetry.

3. The completed figure is called a ______________________ prism. Draw the blocks on the picture below.

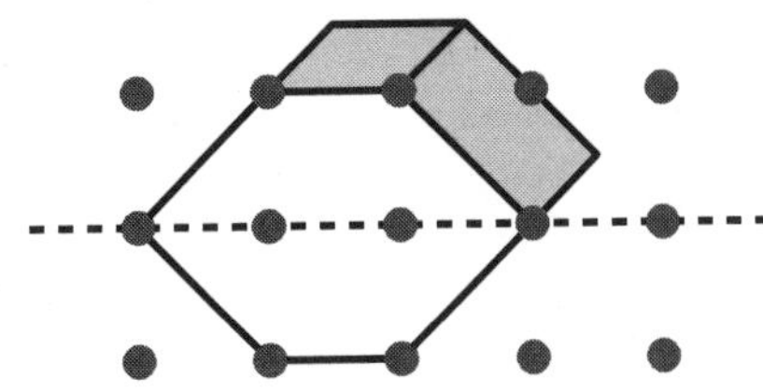

Lines of Symmetry

1. Place four Tangram Blocks as shown.

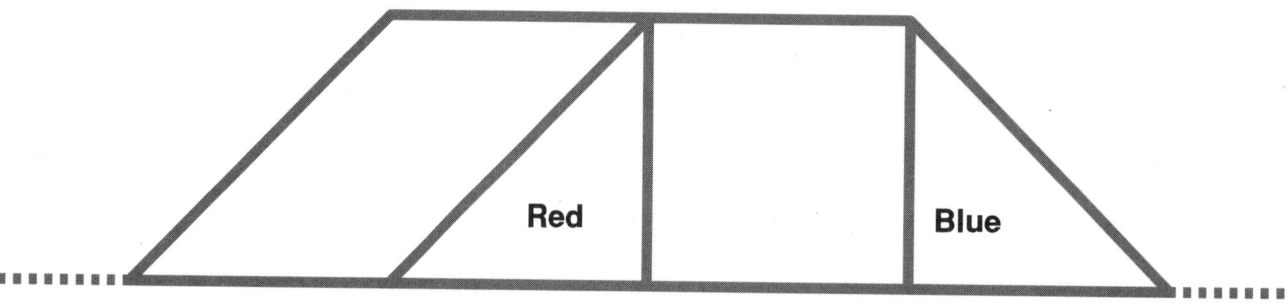

2. Place blocks below the above shape to make the dotted line a line of symmetry.

3. The completed figure is called a ______________________ prism. Draw the blocks on the picture below. Label *R* for red blocks and *B* for blue blocks.

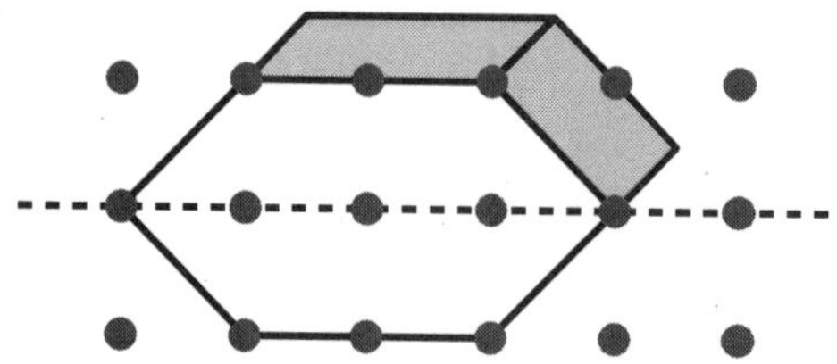

Triangular Prisms

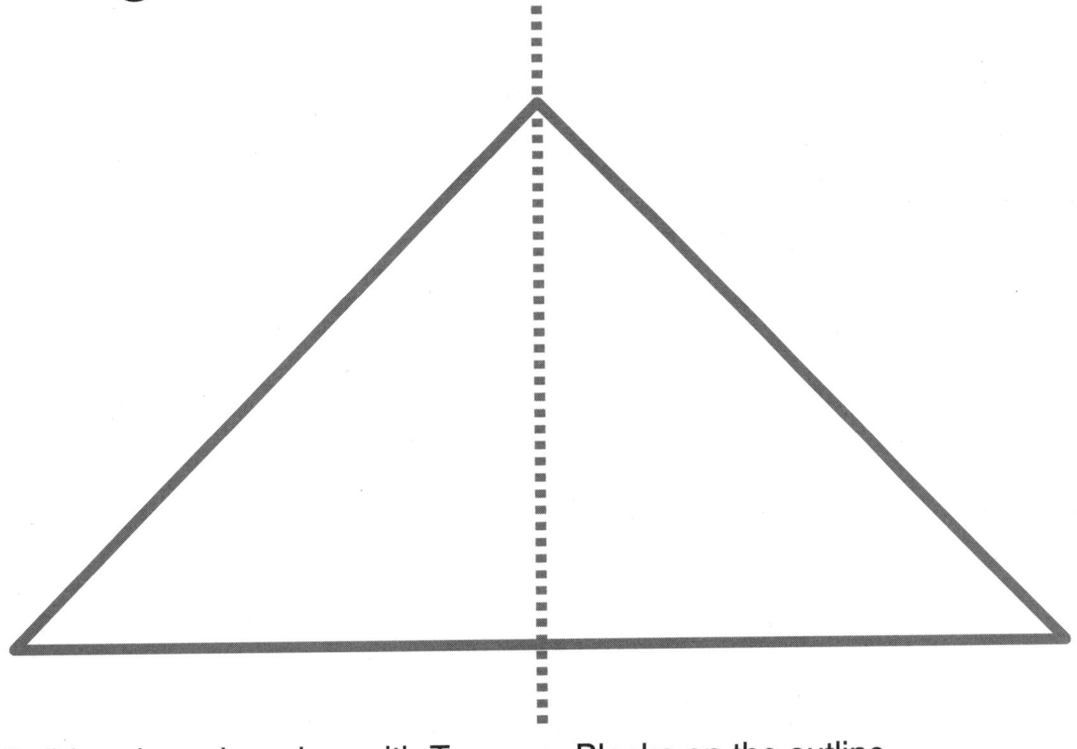

1. Build a triangular prism with Tangram Blocks on the outline above. Make the dotted line a line of symmetry.

   a. Use two blocks.

   b. Use six triangular prisms.

   c. Use six blocks, two must be cubes.

   d. Use six blocks, two must be parallelepipeds.

2. Draw on the pictures below to show answers for b, c, and d. Label *R* for red blocks and *B* for blue blocks.

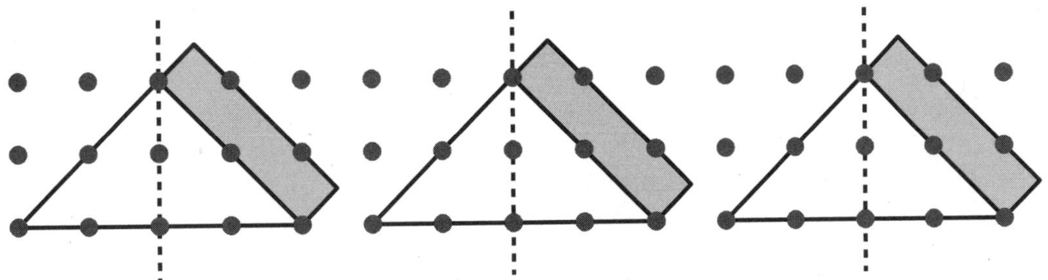

Pentagonal Prisms

1. Build a pentagonal prism with Tangram Blocks on the outline to the right. Make the dotted line a line of symmetry.

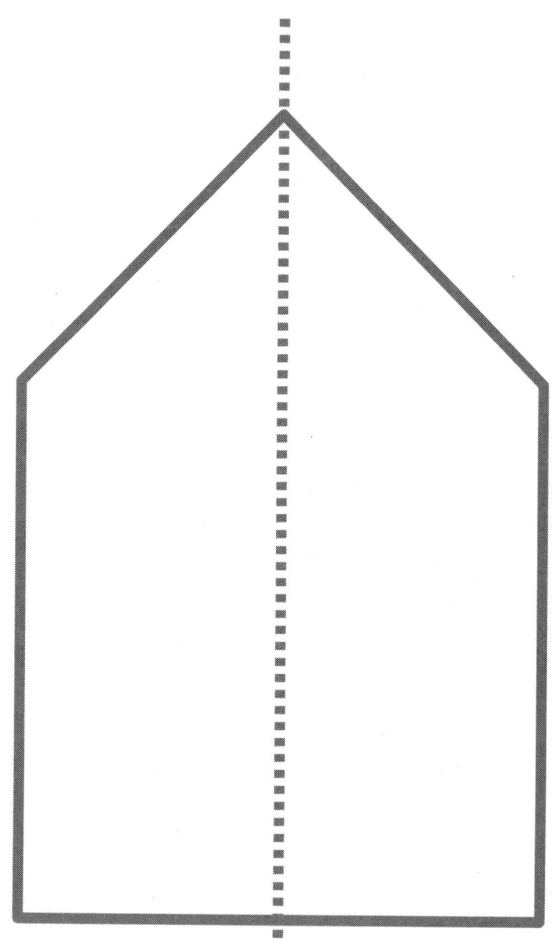

   a. Use two small triangular prisms, two medium triangular prisms, and two cubes.

   b. Use two small triangular prisms, two medium triangular prisms, and two parallelepipeds.

   c. Use one medium triangular prism, two cubes, and two parallelepipeds.

2. Draw on the pictures below to show answers for each problem. Label *R* for red blocks and *B* for blue blocks.

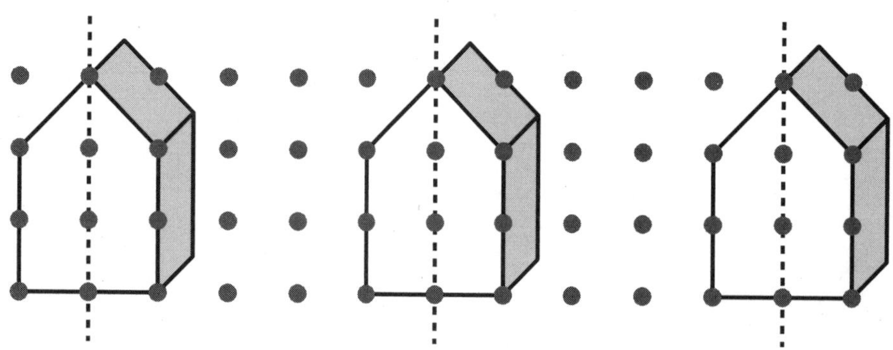

Rectangular Prisms

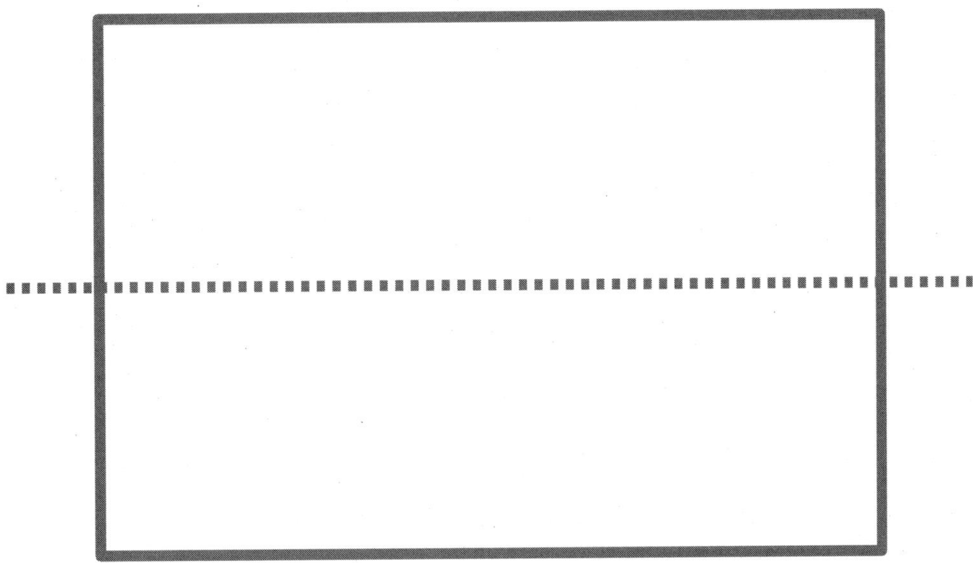

1. Build a rectangular prism with eight Tangram Blocks on the outline above. Make the dotted line a line of symmetry.

   a. Use two cubes, two medium triangular prisms, and four other blocks.

   b. Use two parallelepipeds, two medium triangular prisms, and four other blocks.

   c. Use two cubes, two parallelepipeds, and four other blocks.

2. Draw on the pictures below to show answers for each problem. Label *R* for red blocks and *B* for blue blocks.

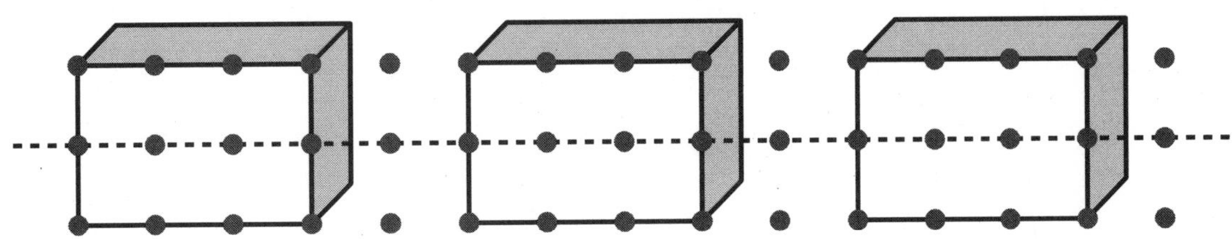

Rectangular Prisms

Use ten Tangram Blocks (all except the four large triangular prisms).

1. On the outline at the right, build rectangular prisms like the ones started below. Make the dotted line a line of symmetry.

2. Draw on the pictures below to show answers for each of the rectangular prisms. Label *R* for red blocks and *B* for blue blocks.

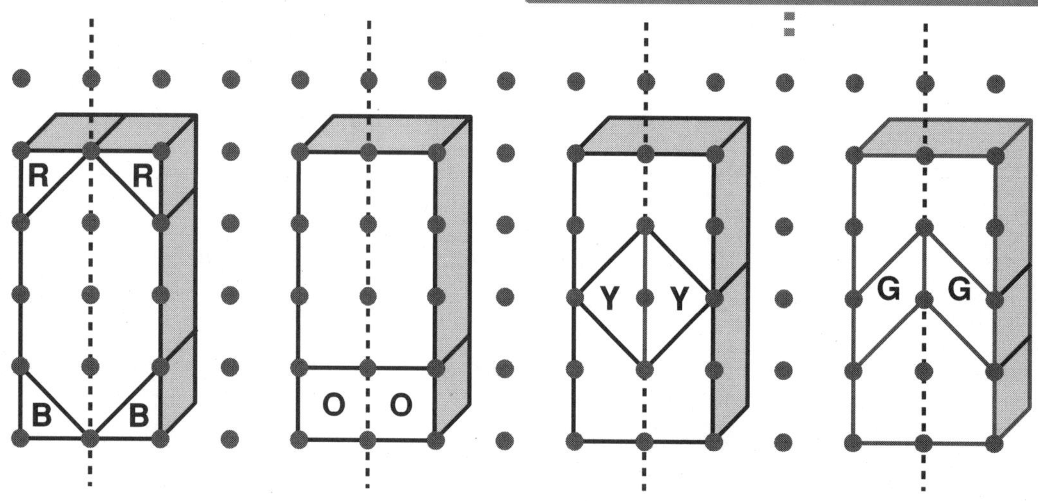

Heptagonal Prisms

Use eight or ten Tangram Blocks.

1. Build two different heptagonal prisms on the outline. Make the dotted line a line of symmetry.

2. Draw on these pictures to show each of the heptagonal prisms. Label *R* for red blocks and *B* for blue blocks.

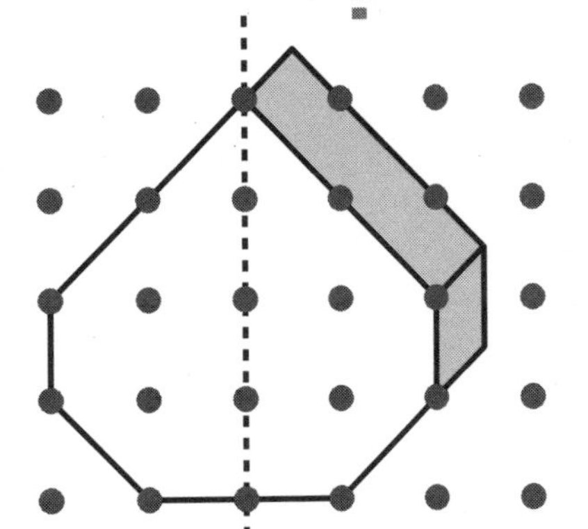

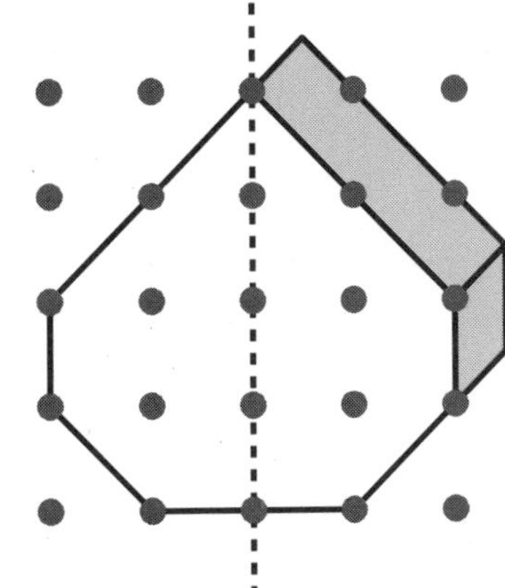

Octagonal Prisms

Use 12 Tangram Blocks.

1. Build octagonal prisms on the outline. Make the dotted line a line of symmetry.
   a. Use all blocks except the two parallelepipeds.
   b. Use all blocks except the two cubes.
   c. Use all blocks except the two medium triangular prisms.
2. Draw on the pictures to show answers for each problem. Label *R* for red blocks and *B* for blue blocks.

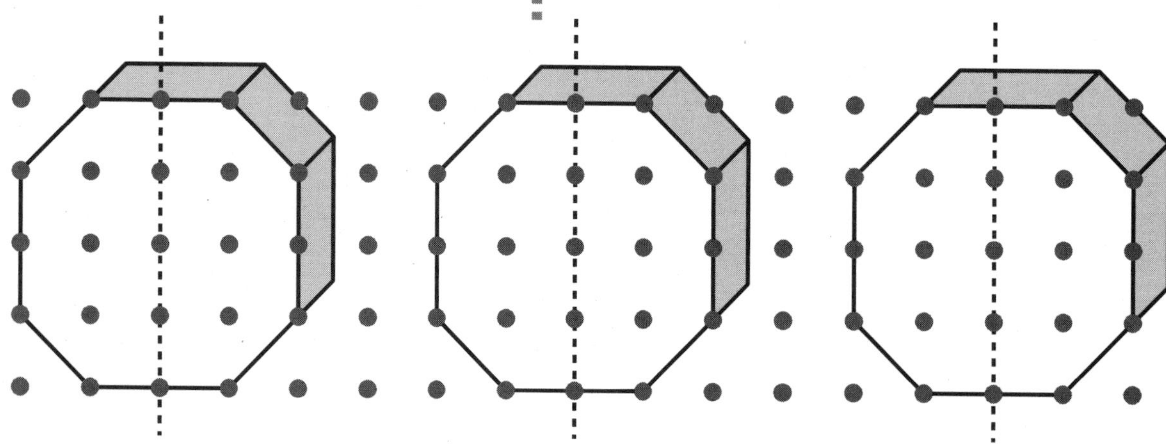

Square Prisms

Use these Tangram Blocks: four large triangular prisms.

1. Build a square prism on the outline so like colors do not touch at matching faces.

Some shapes have more than one line of symmetry.

2. How many lines of symmetry are there on this square prism? __________

3. Draw on the picture to show the blocks and lines of symmetry. Label *R* for red blocks and *B* for blue blocks.

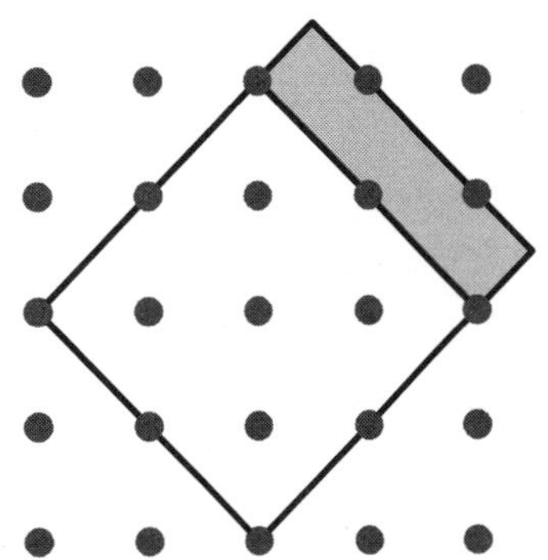

Square Prisms

Use these Tangram Blocks: three large triangular prisms, two small triangular prisms, and one cube.

1. Build a square prism on the outline so like colors do not touch at matching faces. There are two ways to do this.

2. Draw on the pictures to show the blocks and lines of symmetry. Label *R* for red blocks and *B* for blue blocks.

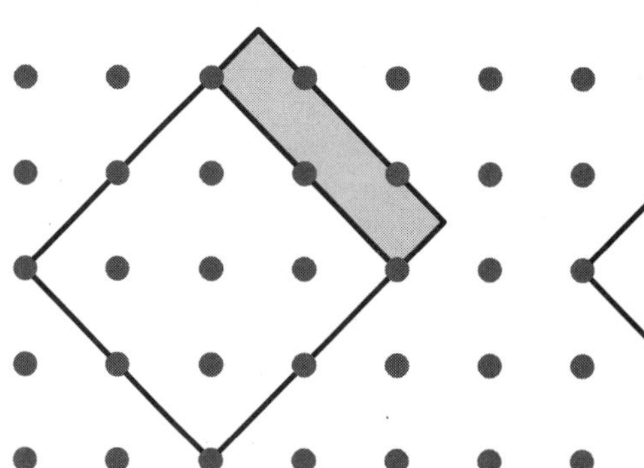

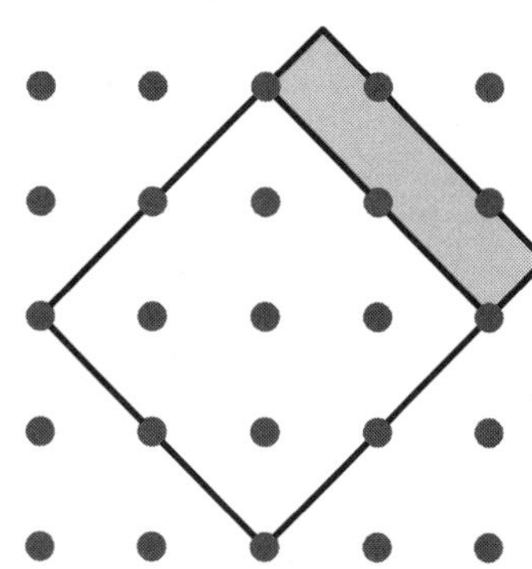

Square Prisms

Use these Tangram Blocks:
two large triangular prisms,
four small triangular prisms,
and two cubes.

1. Build a square prism on the outline so like colors do not touch at matching faces.

2. Draw on the picture to show the blocks and line of symmetry. Label *R* for red blocks and *B* for blue blocks.

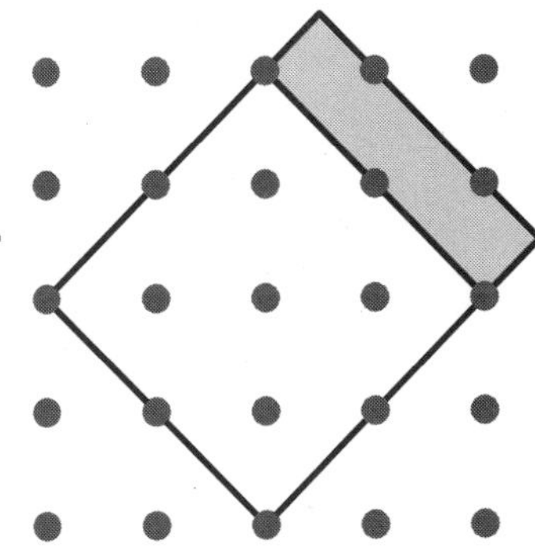

Square Prisms

Use these Tangram Blocks: two large triangular prisms, two medium triangular prisms, and four small triangular prisms.

1. Build a square prism on the outline. Like colors may touch at matching faces.

2. Draw on the picture to show the blocks and line of symmetry. Label *R* for red blocks and *B* for blue blocks.

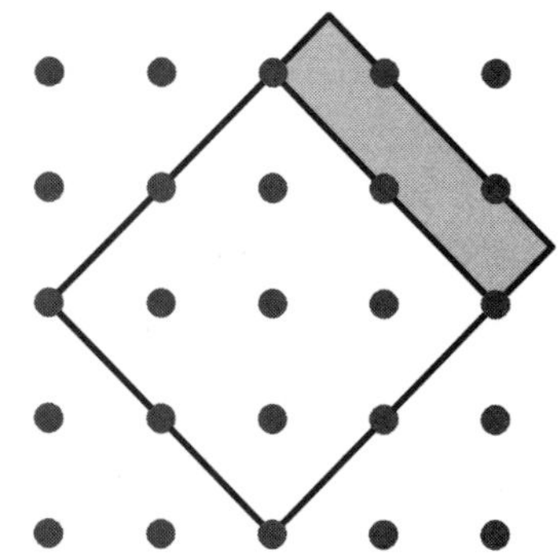

Square Prisms

1. Build square prisms with Tangram Blocks on the outline so there is one line of symmetry.

   Like colors may touch at matching faces.

   a. Use five blocks.

   b. Use seven blocks.

   c. Use nine blocks.

2. Draw on the pictures to show the blocks and lines of symmetry. Label *R* for red blocks and *B* for blue blocks.

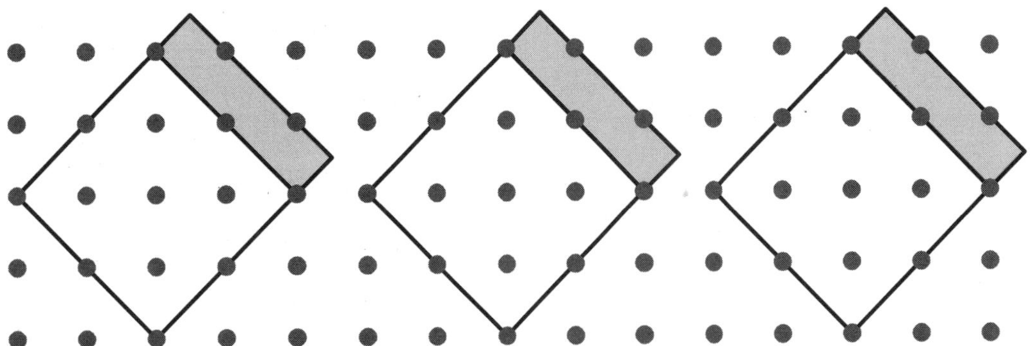

Square Prisms

Use ten Tangram Blocks (all except the four large triangular prisms).

1. Build a square prism on the outline. Like colors may touch at matching faces.

2. Draw on the picture to show the blocks and line of symmetry. Label *R* for red blocks and *B* for blue blocks.

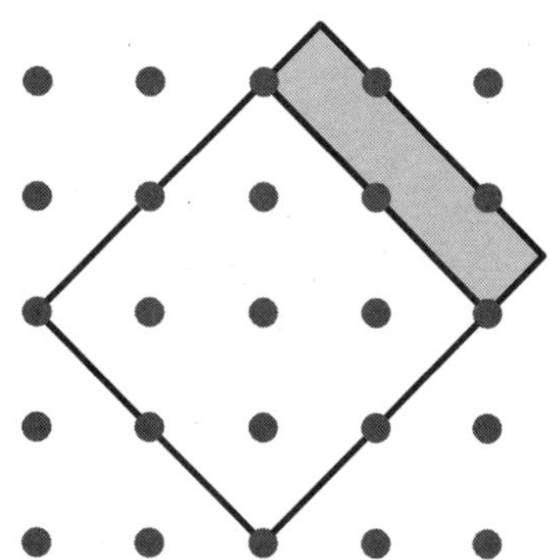

Chapter 5

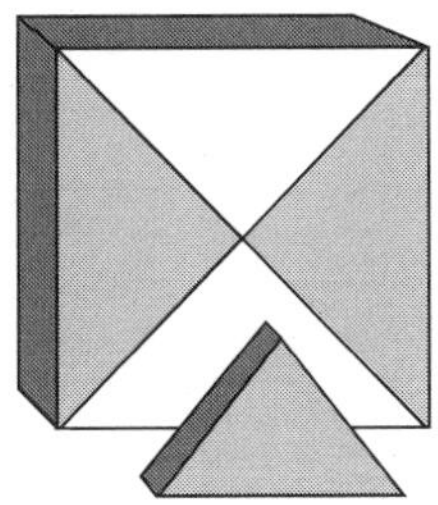

Puzzles and Designs

Overview

In this last section, students use all 14 Tangram Blocks to create each figure. Activities 1–14 require keeping like colors apart. In activities 15–21, like colors may or may not touch at matching faces. The four animals in Puzzles and Designs 8–14 cannot be easily drawn on dot paper. Do not encourage students to try to draw them.

Students will have the opportunity in Activities 1–14 to create 16 animal patterns. They begin by simply placing the blocks on full-size outlines. Then using smaller outlines on dot paper as guides, students construct the figures on their desks. Finally, even smaller outlines on plain paper serve as guides for their work at their desks.

Activities 15–21 have students create block designs by putting the blocks together in a prescribed order. Students count the number of vertical sides of a completed figure with the addition of each block. They record this information in a table. Students are encouraged to look for patterns within the table.

You may notice the following while observing students working on this section.

- Students delight in using problem-solving skills to build the various animals.
- Some add to the menagerie by creating their own animal shapes, even though they may not be easily recorded on dot paper. (Note: Some of the patterns in this book were created by students.)
- Even at the kindergarten level, some students are able to easily count the vertical sides in Activities 15–21.

Lion

Use all 14 Tangram Blocks.

Place the blocks on the outline. Like colors may not touch at matching faces.

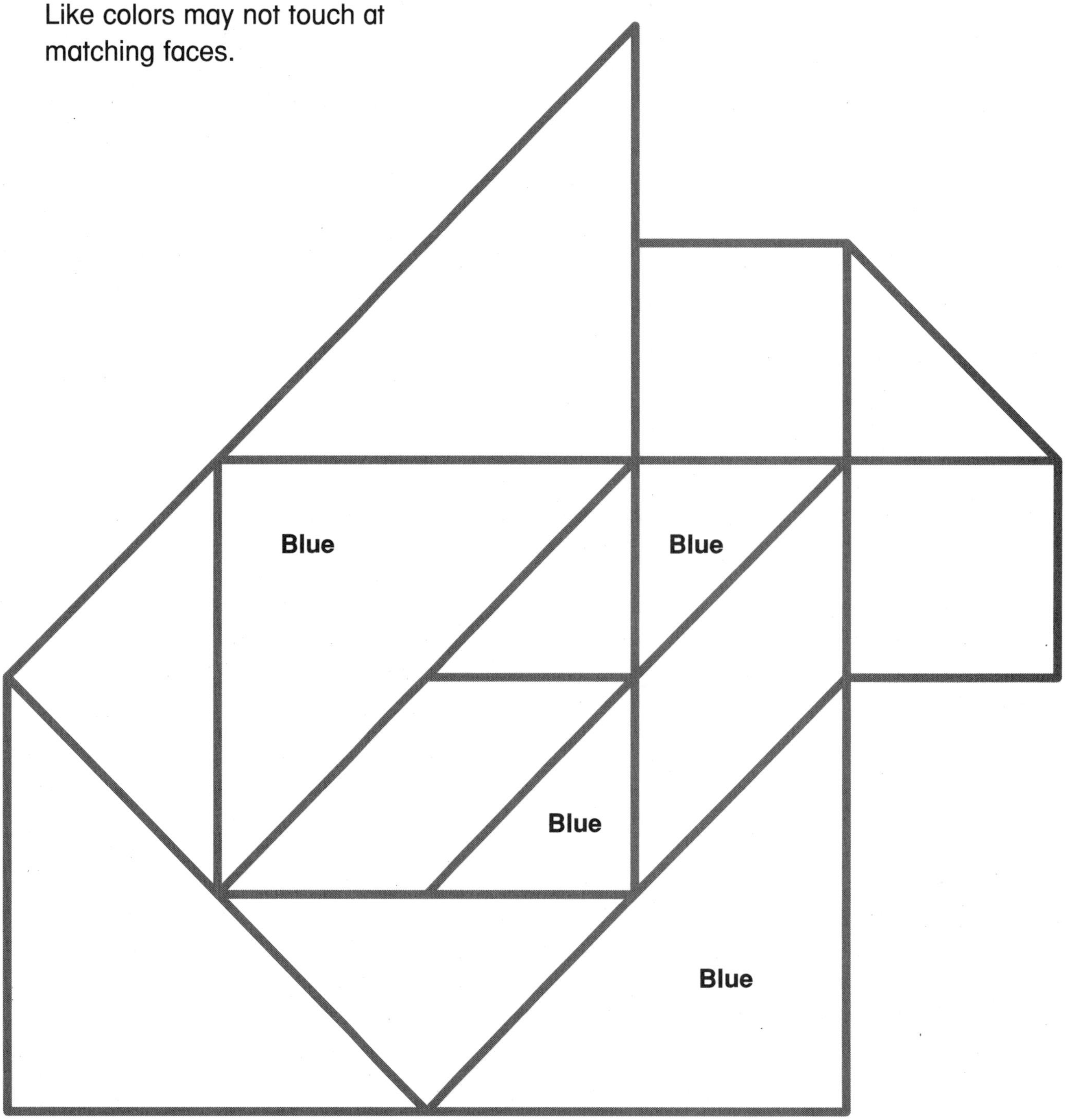

Blue

Blue

Blue

Blue

Swan

Use all 14 Tangram Blocks. Place the blocks on the outline.
Like colors may not touch at matching faces.

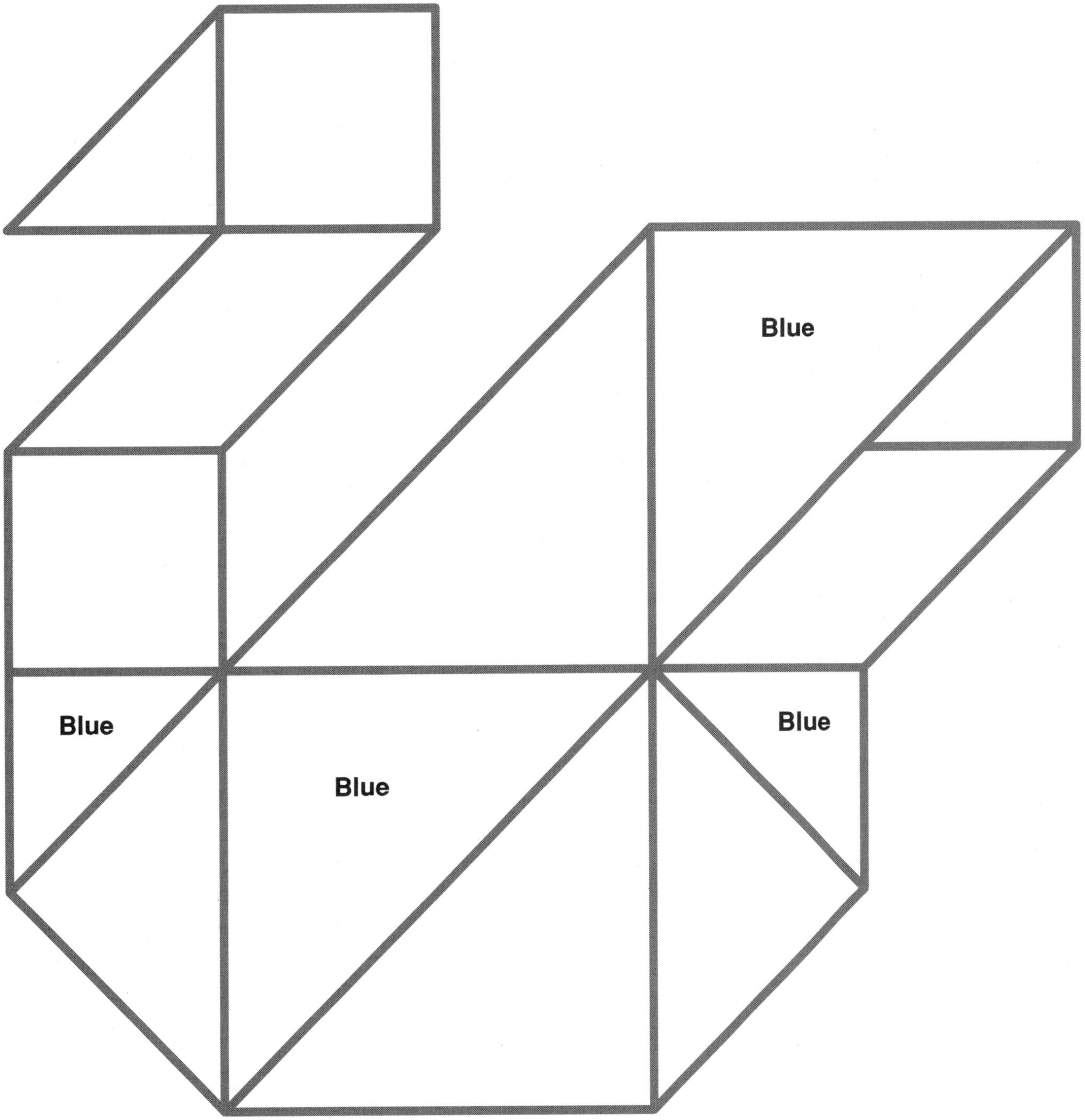

Blue

Blue

Blue

Blue

Puppy

Use all 14 Tangram Blocks.

Arrange the blocks to form a puppy *like* the one below.
Like colors may not touch at matching faces.

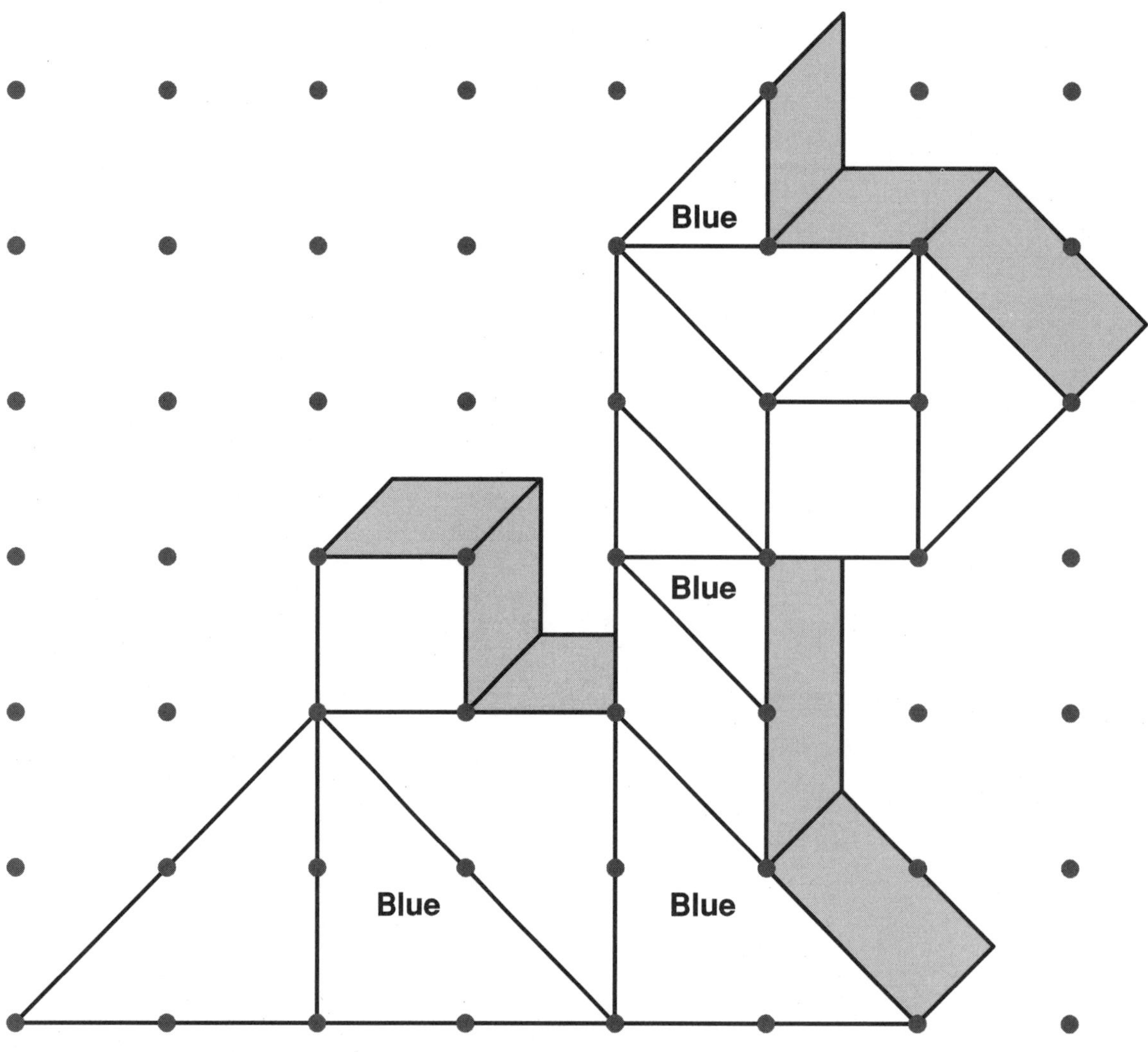

Pig and Turtle

Use all 14 Tangram Blocks for each animal.

Arrange the blocks to form a pig shape and a turtle shape like the ones below. Like colors may not touch at matching faces.

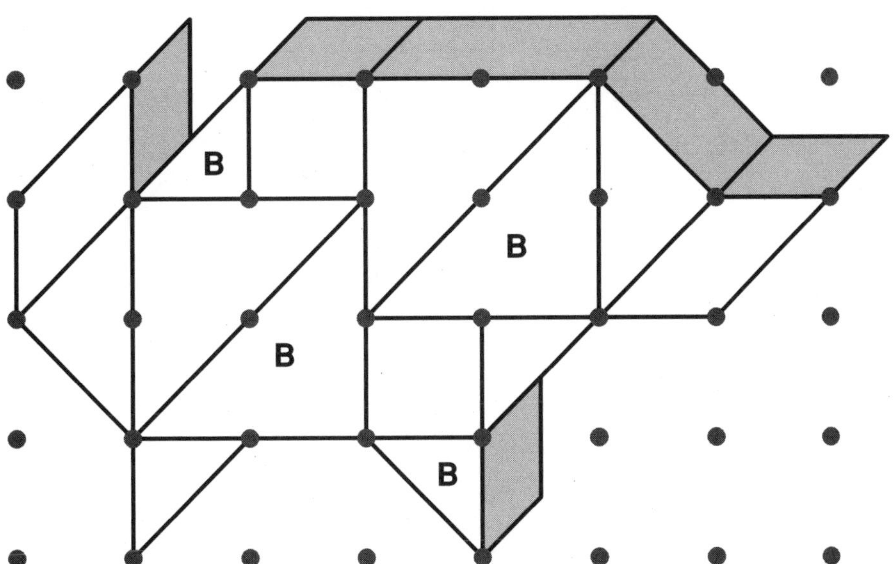

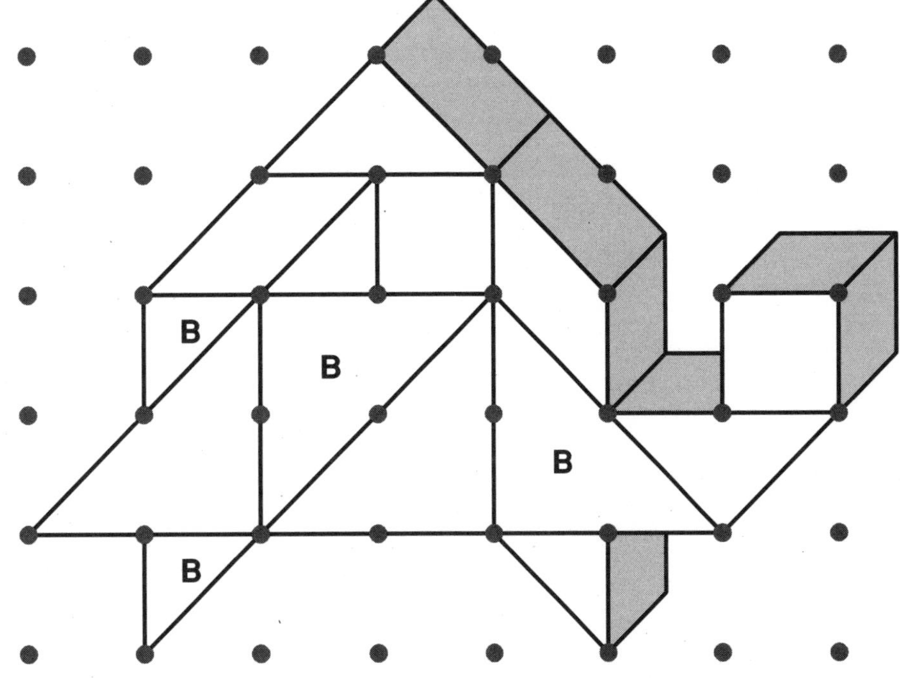

Snail

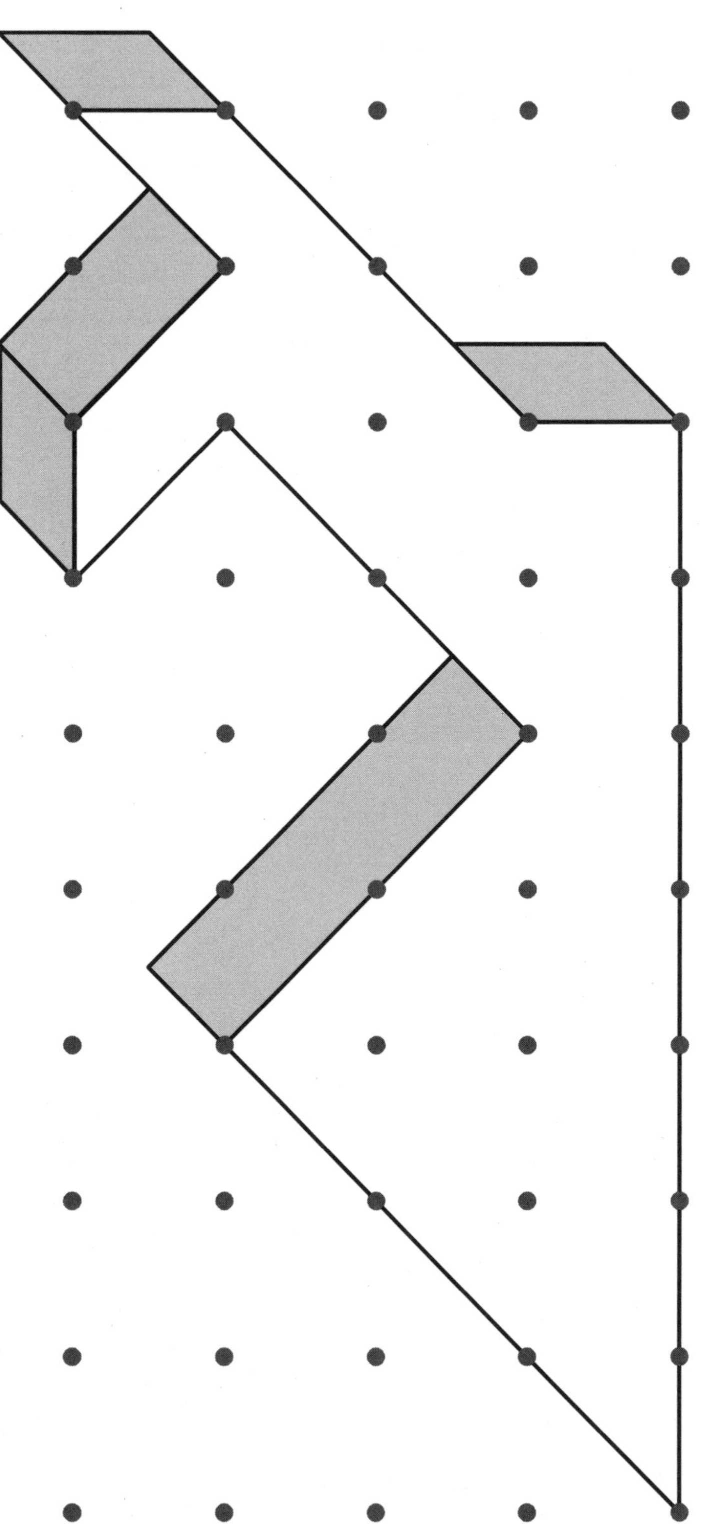

Use all 14 Tangram Blocks.

Arrange the blocks to form a snail shape like the one to the right. Like colors may not touch at matching faces.

Draw on the picture to show the placement of the blocks. Label the blue blocks with the letter *B*.

Flying Duck

Use all 14 Tangram Blocks.

Arrange the blocks to form a flying duck shape like the one below. Like colors may not touch at matching faces. Draw on the picture to show the placement of the blocks. Label the blue blocks with the letter *B*.

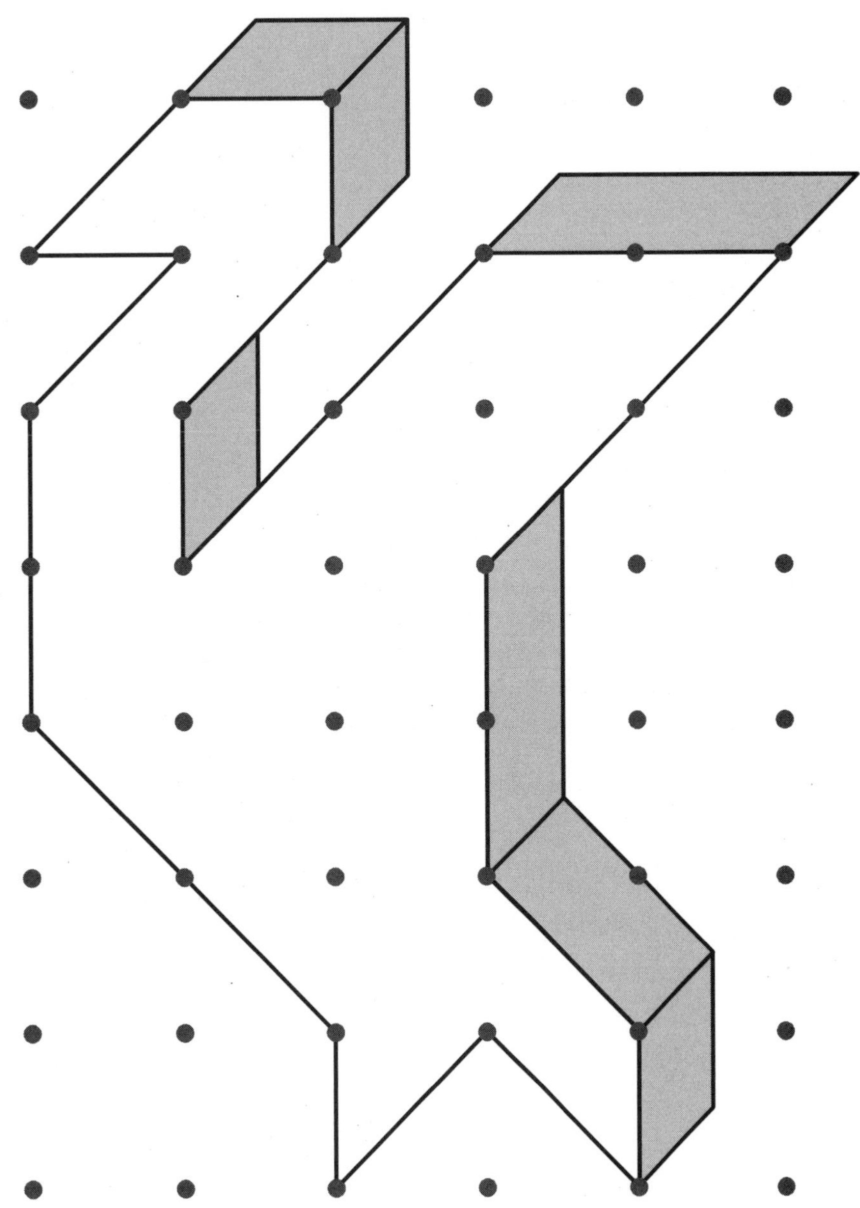

Critter and Pointer

Use all 14 Tangram Blocks for each animal.

Arrange the blocks to form a critter shape and a pointer shape like the ones shown. Like colors may not touch at matching faces. Draw on the pictures to show the placement of the blocks. Label the blue blocks with the letter *B*.

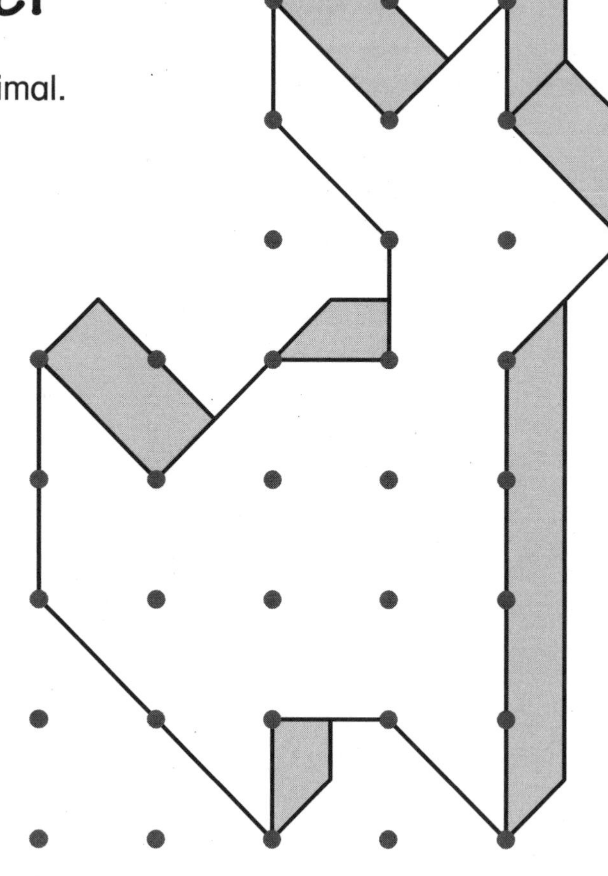

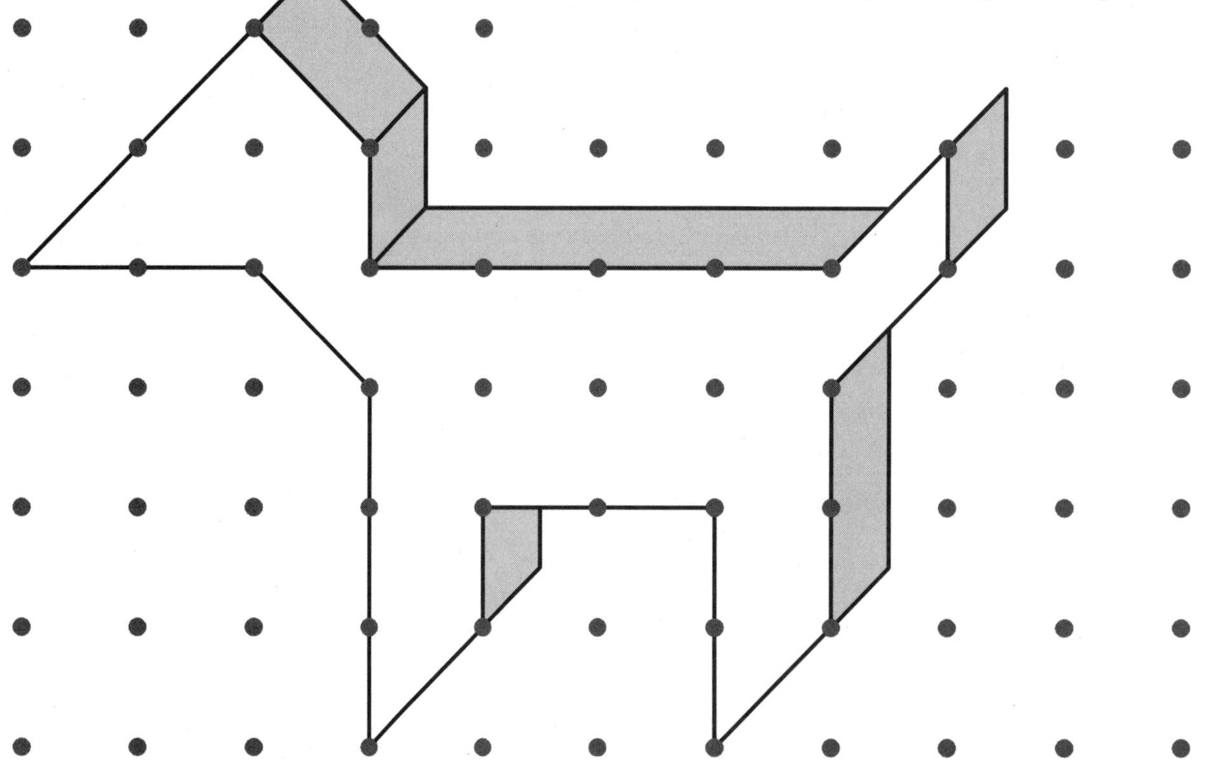

Schnauzer

Use all 14 Tangram Blocks.

Arrange the blocks to form a schnauzer shape like the one below. Like colors may not touch at matching faces. Note: This design uses turned blocks that would not line up on dot paper. You do not need to draw the blocks on dot paper or on the outline.

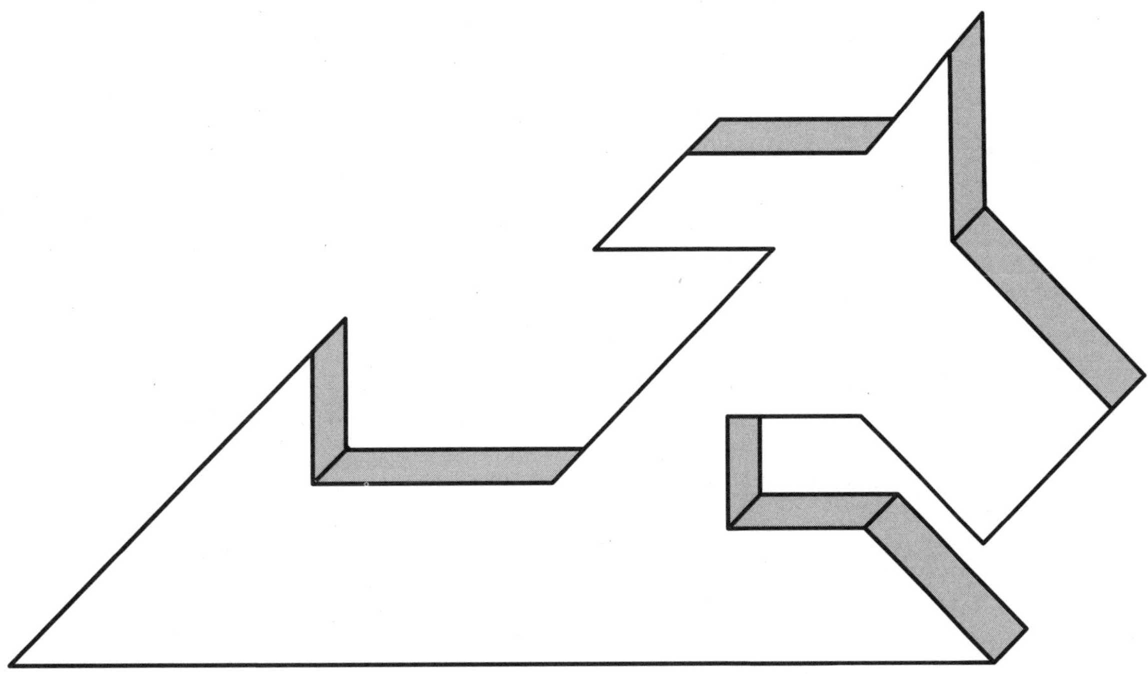

Parrot

Use all 14 Tangram Blocks.

Arrange the blocks to form a parrot shape like the one below. Like colors may not touch at matching faces. Note: This design uses turned blocks that would not line up on dot paper. You do not need to draw the blocks on dot paper or on the outline.

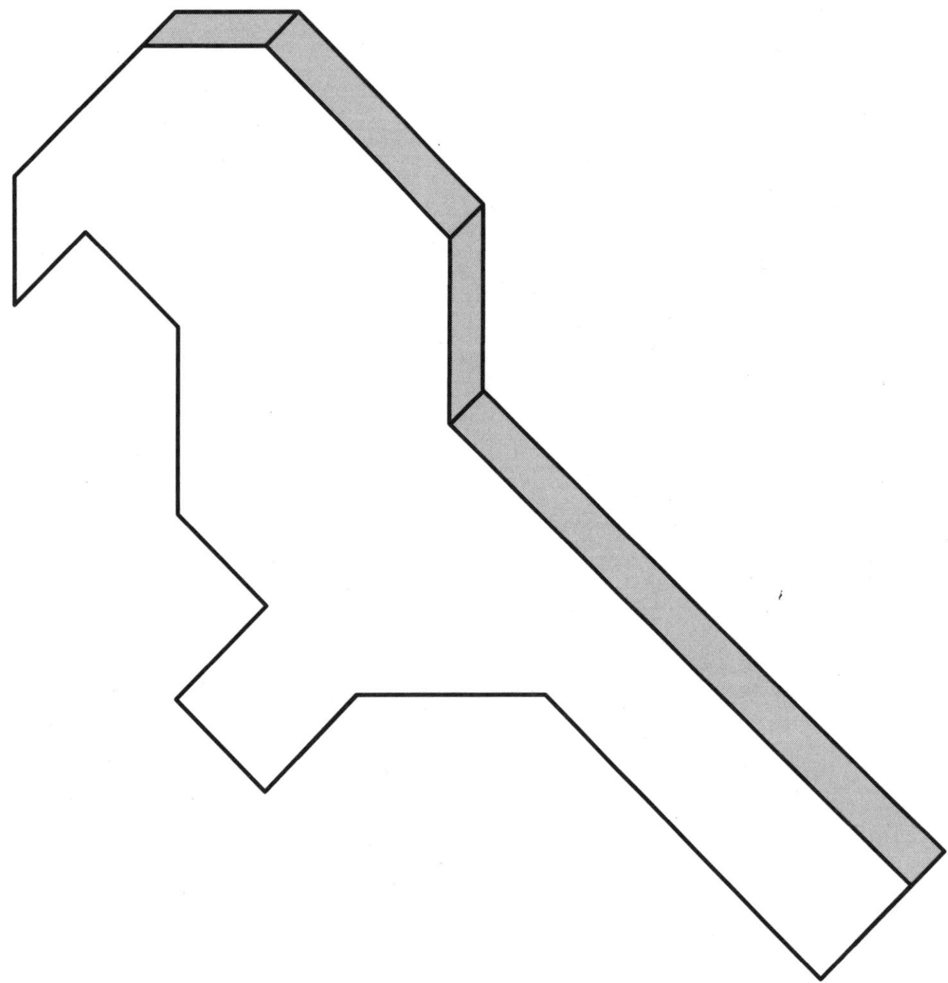

Bunny

Use all 14 Tangram Blocks.

Arrange the blocks to form a bunny shape like the one below. Like colors may not touch at matching faces. Note: This design uses turned blocks that would not line up on dot paper. You do not need to draw the blocks on dot paper or on the outline.

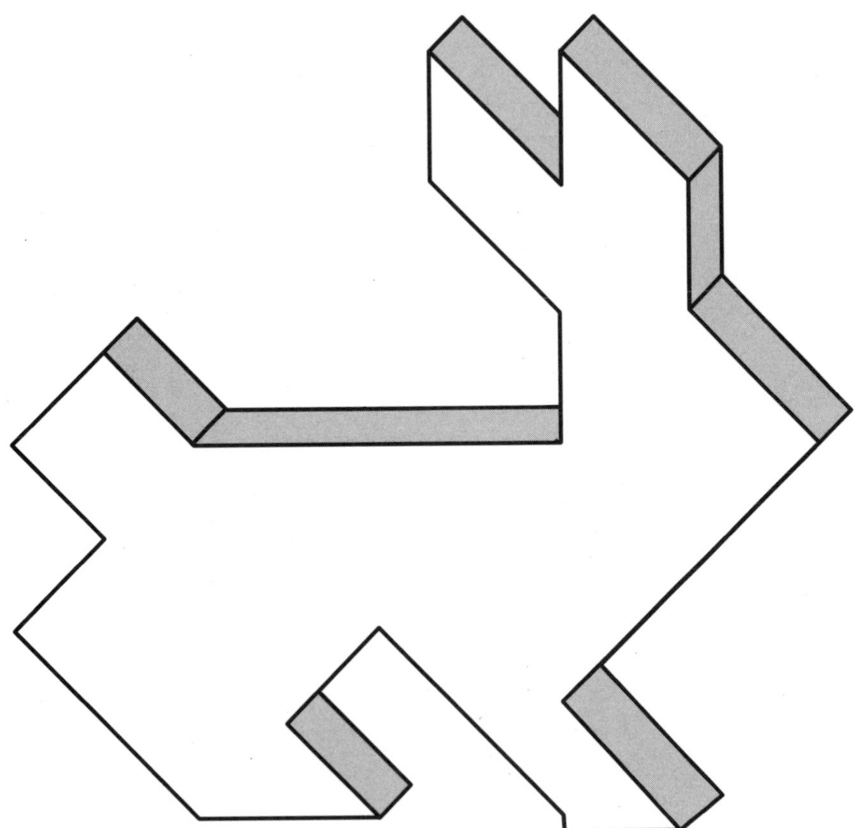

Kangaroo

Use all 14 Tangram Blocks.

Arrange the blocks to form a kangaroo shape like the one below. Like colors may not touch at matching faces. Note: This design uses turned blocks that would not line up on dot paper. You do not need to draw the blocks on dot paper or on the outline.

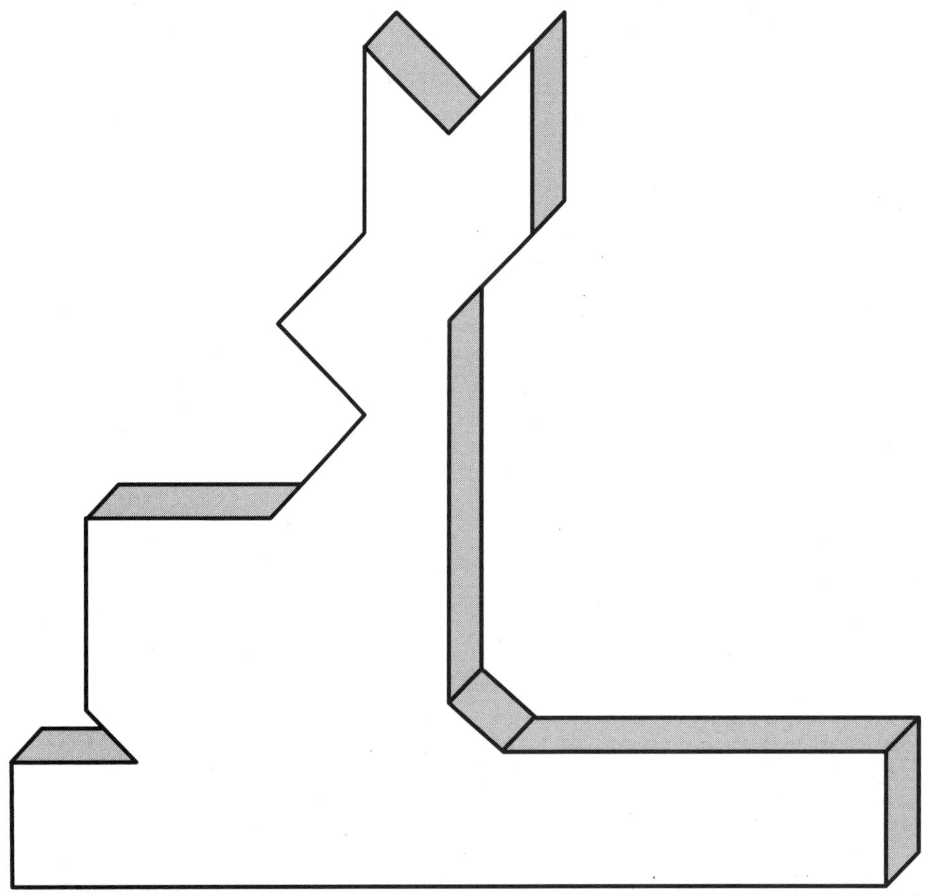

Whale

Use all 14 Tangram Blocks.

Arrange the blocks to form a whale shape like the one below. Like colors may not touch at matching faces. Note: This design uses turned blocks that would not line up on dot paper. You do not need to draw the blocks on dot paper or on the outline.

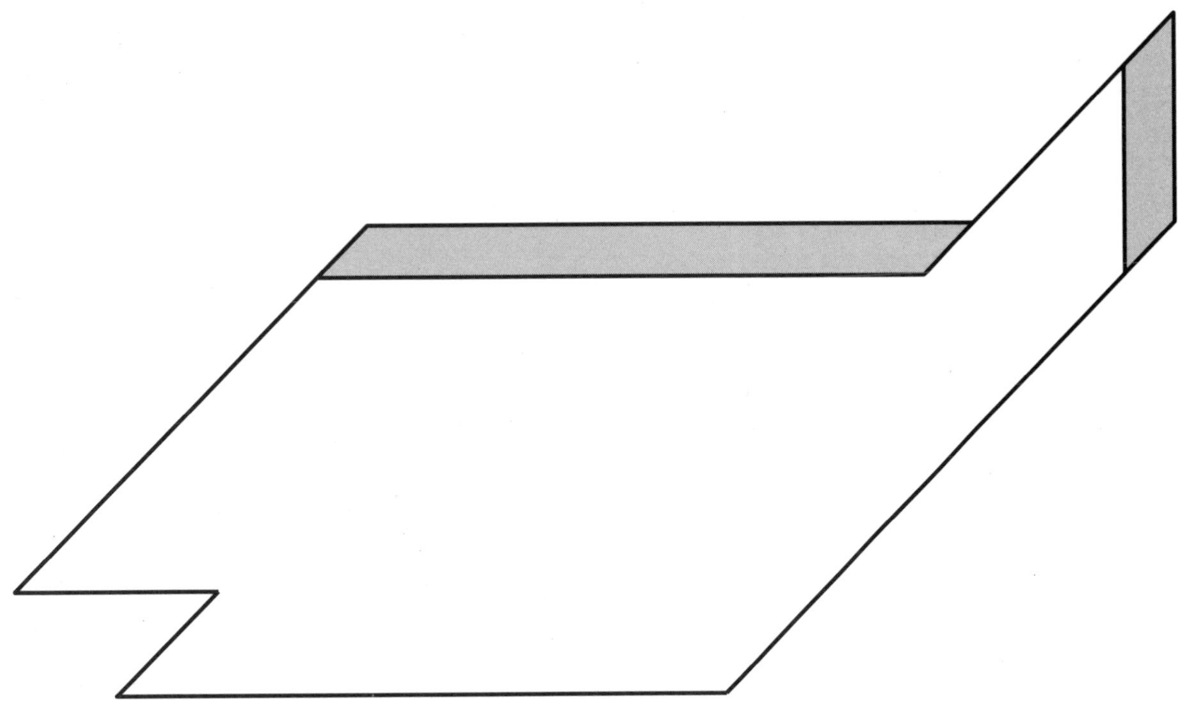

Fox

Use all 14 Tangram Blocks.

Arrange the blocks to form a fox shape like the one below. Like colors may not touch at matching faces. Note: This design uses turned blocks that would not line up on dot paper. You do not need to draw the blocks on dot paper or on the outline.

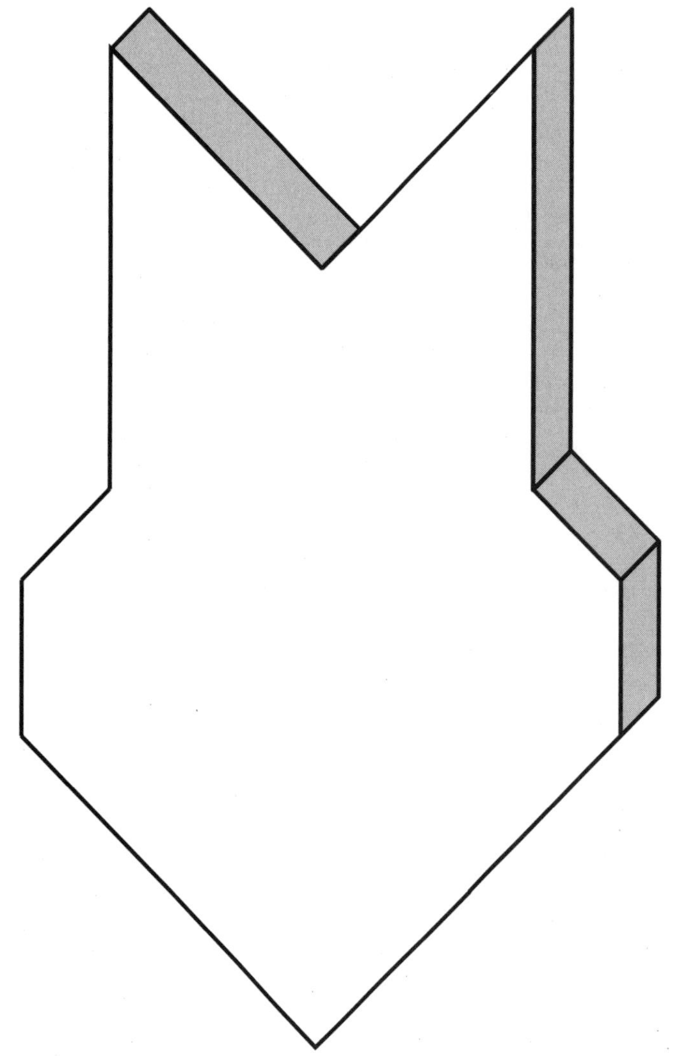

Cat

Use all 14 Tangram Blocks.

Arrange the blocks to form a cat shape like the one below. Like colors may not touch at matching faces. Note: This design uses turned blocks that would not line up on dot paper. You do not need to draw the blocks on dot paper or on the outline.

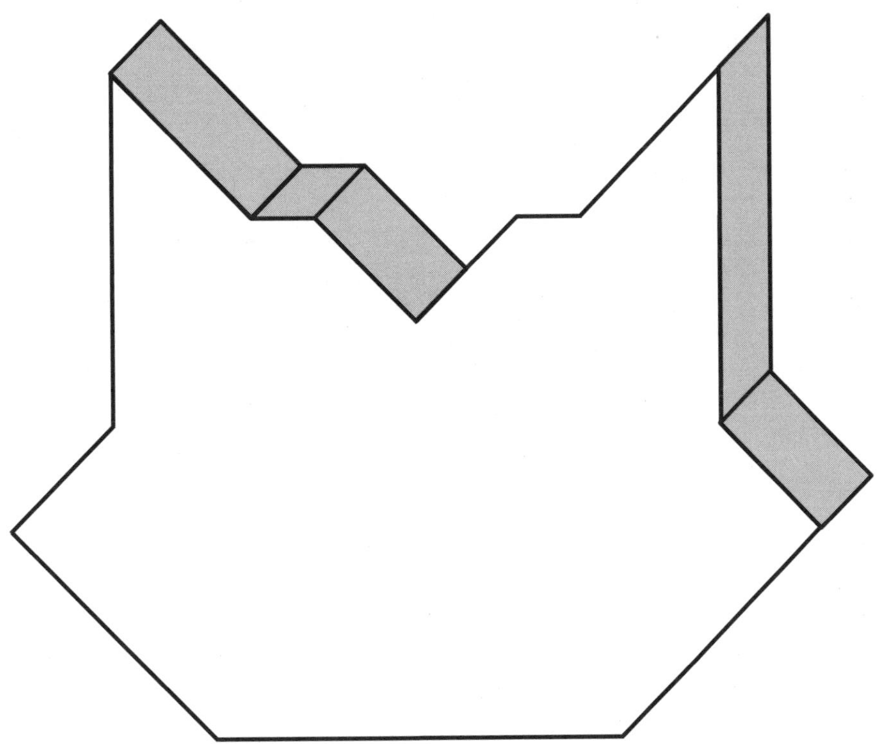

Counting Vertical Sides

Place the Tangram Blocks one at a time in the order shown on the diagram. After you put each block down, count the number of straight vertical sides. Sometimes the new block just makes one vertical side longer. So be careful to count the new, longer side as still one side. Complete the table.

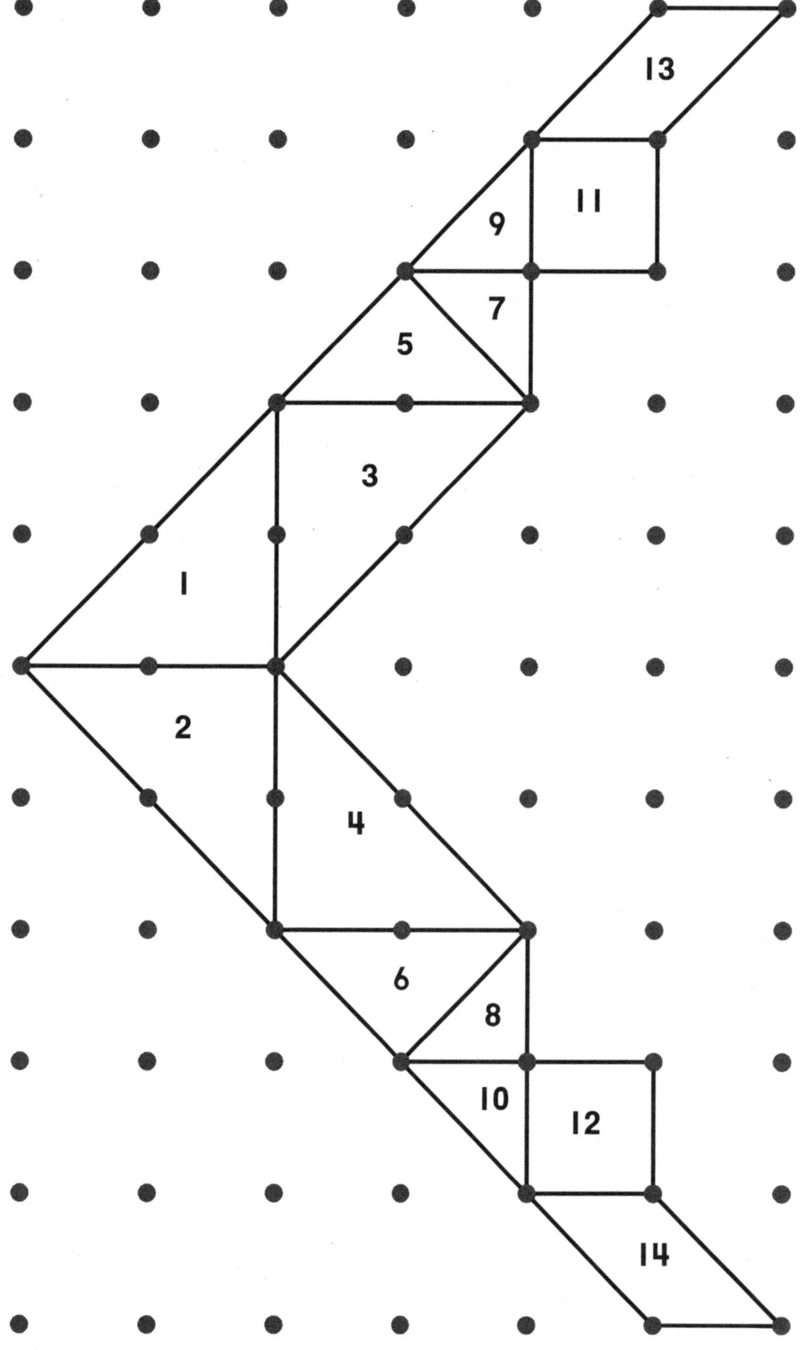

Blocks	Vertical Sides
1	3
2	3
3	
4	
5	
6	
7	
8	
9	
10	
11	
12	
13	
14	

What patterns did you find as you added the blocks?

____

____

Counting Vertical Sides

Place the Tangram Blocks one at a time in the order shown on the diagram. After you put each block down, count the number of straight vertical sides. Sometimes the new block just makes one vertical side longer. So be careful to count the new, longer side as still one side. Complete the table.

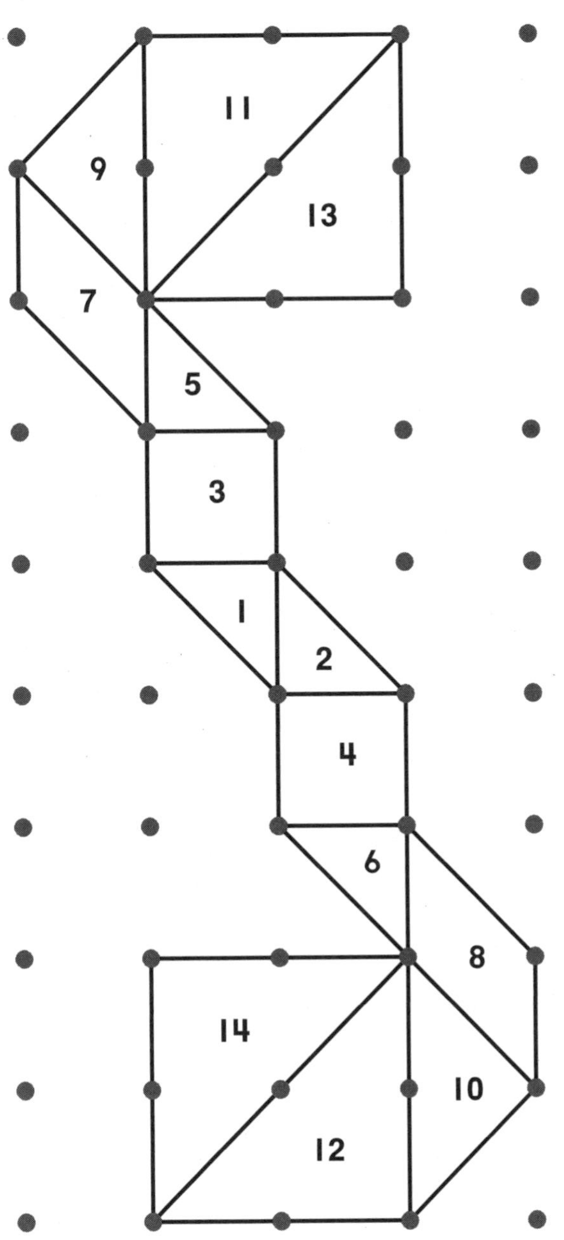

Blocks	Vertical Sides
1	
2	
3	
4	
5	
6	
7	
8	
9	
10	
11	
12	
13	
14	

What patterns did you find as you added the blocks?

____

____

Counting Vertical Sides

Place the Tangram Blocks one at a time in the order shown on the diagram. After you put each block down, count the number of straight vertical sides. Sometimes the new block just makes one vertical side longer. So be careful to count the new, longer side as still one side. Complete the table.

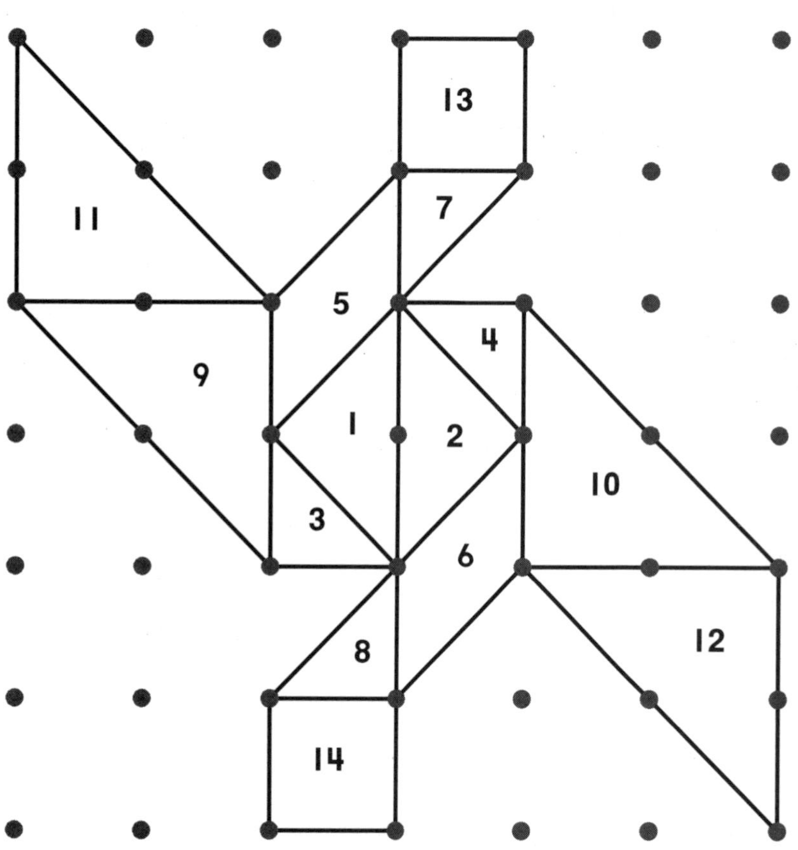

Blocks	Vertical Sides
1	
2	
3	
4	
5	
6	
7	
8	
9	
10	
11	
12	
13	
14	

What patterns did you find as you added the blocks?

____

____

Counting Vertical Sides

Place the Tangram Blocks one at a time in the order shown on the diagram. After you put each block down, count the number of straight vertical sides. Sometimes the new block just makes one vertical side longer. So be careful to count the new, longer side as still one side. Complete the table.

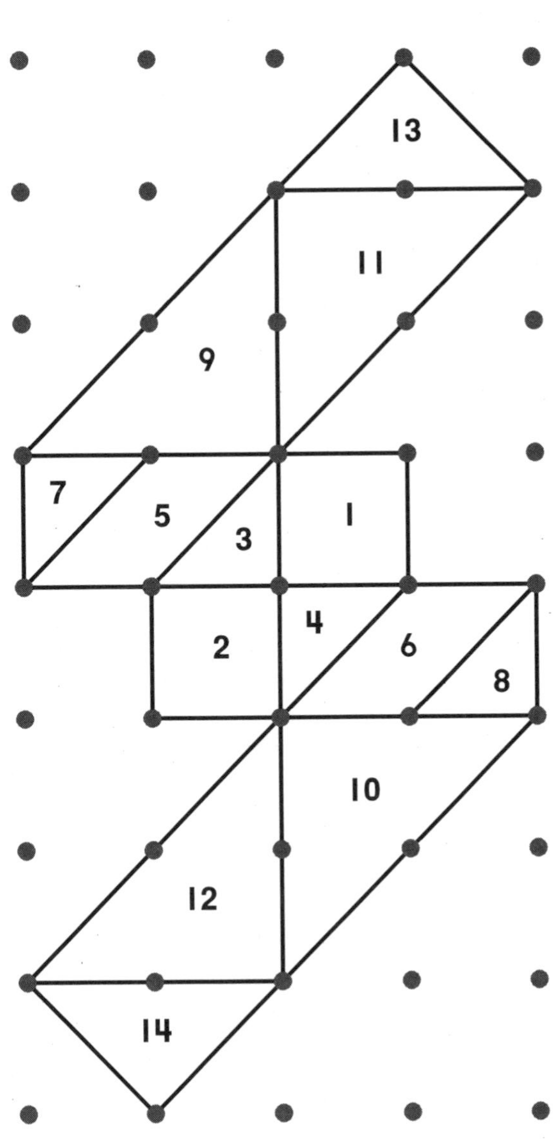

Blocks	Vertical Sides
1	
2	
3	
4	
5	
6	
7	
8	
9	
10	
11	
12	
13	
14	

What patterns did you find as you added the blocks?

____

____

Counting Vertical Sides

Place the Tangram Blocks one at a time in the order shown on the diagram. After you put each block down, count the number of straight vertical sides. Sometimes the new block just makes one vertical side longer. So be careful to count the new, longer side as still one side. Complete the table.

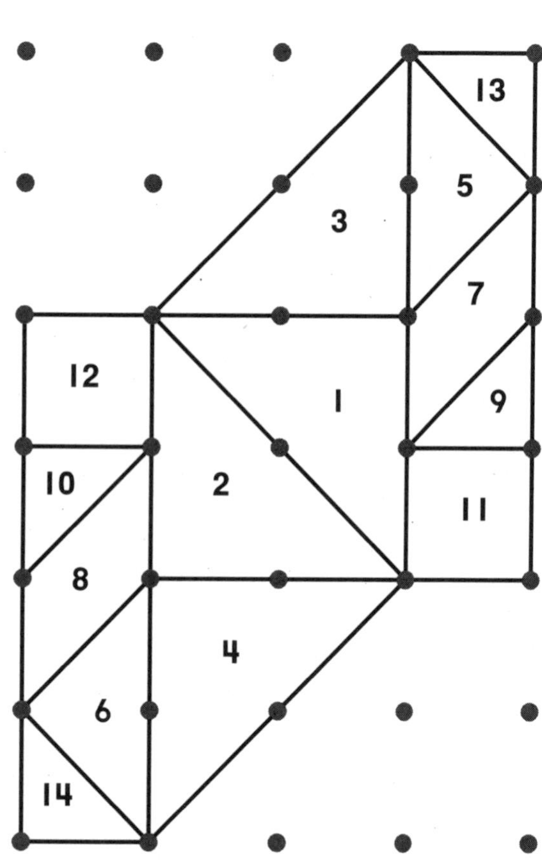

Blocks	Vertical Sides
1	
2	
3	
4	
5	
6	
7	
8	
9	
10	
11	
12	
13	
14	

What patterns did you find as you added the blocks?

____

____

Counting Vertical Sides

Place the Tangram Blocks one at a time in the order shown on the diagram. After you put each block down, count the number of straight vertical sides. Sometimes the new block just makes one vertical side longer. So be careful to count the new, longer side as still one side. Complete the table.

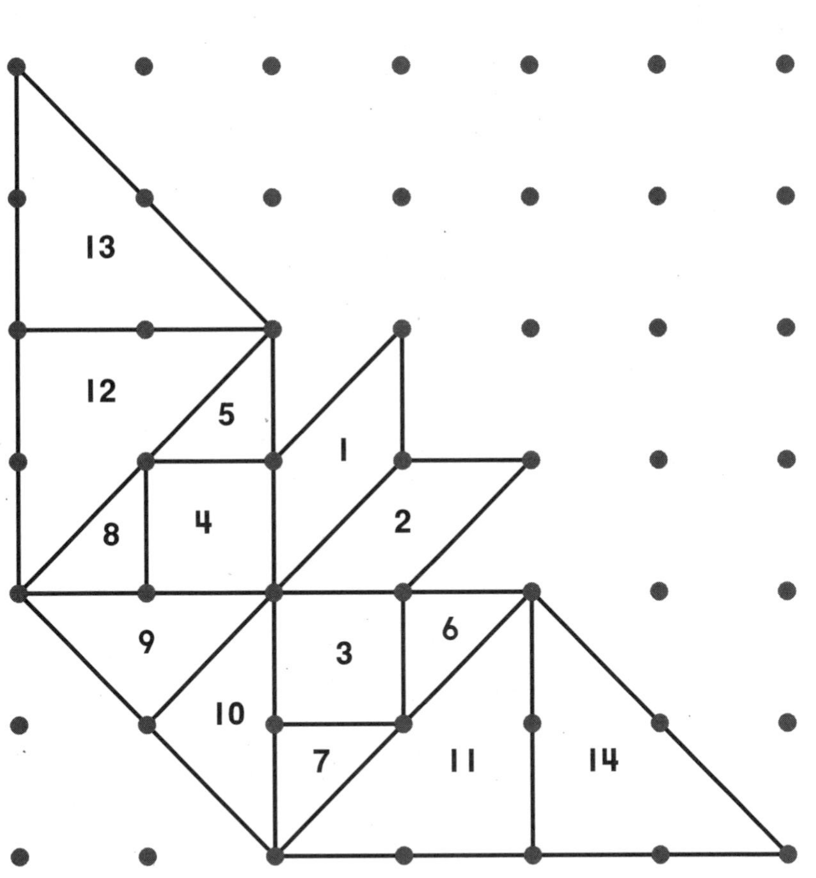

Blocks	Vertical Sides
1	
2	
3	
4	
5	
6	
7	
8	
9	
10	
11	
12	
13	
14	

What patterns did you find as you added the blocks?

____

____

Counting Vertical Sides

Place the Tangram Blocks one at a time in the order shown on the diagram. After you put each block down, count the number of straight vertical sides. Sometimes the new block just makes one vertical side longer. So be careful to count the new, longer side as still one side. Complete the table.

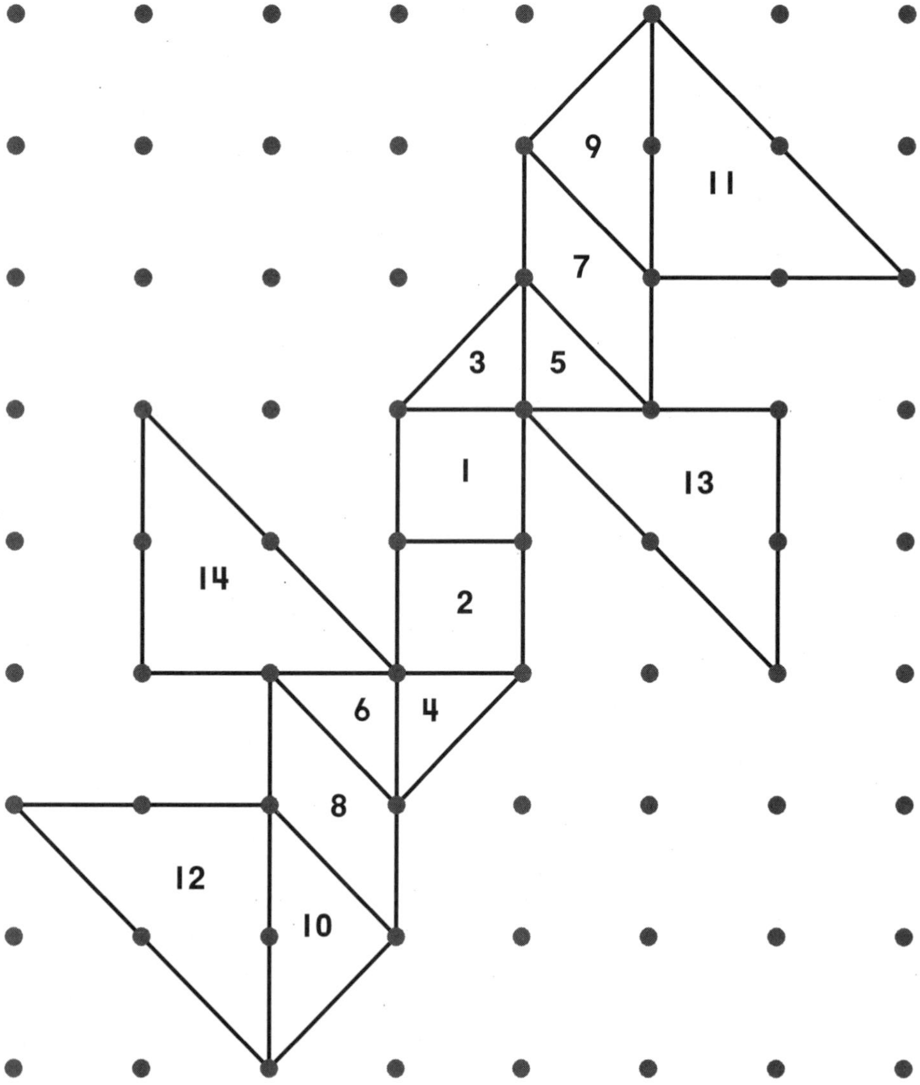

Blocks	Vertical Sides
1	
2	
3	
4	
5	
6	
7	
8	
9	
10	
11	
12	
13	
14	

What patterns did you find as you added the blocks?

Recording Numerals (Block Figures 16–25)

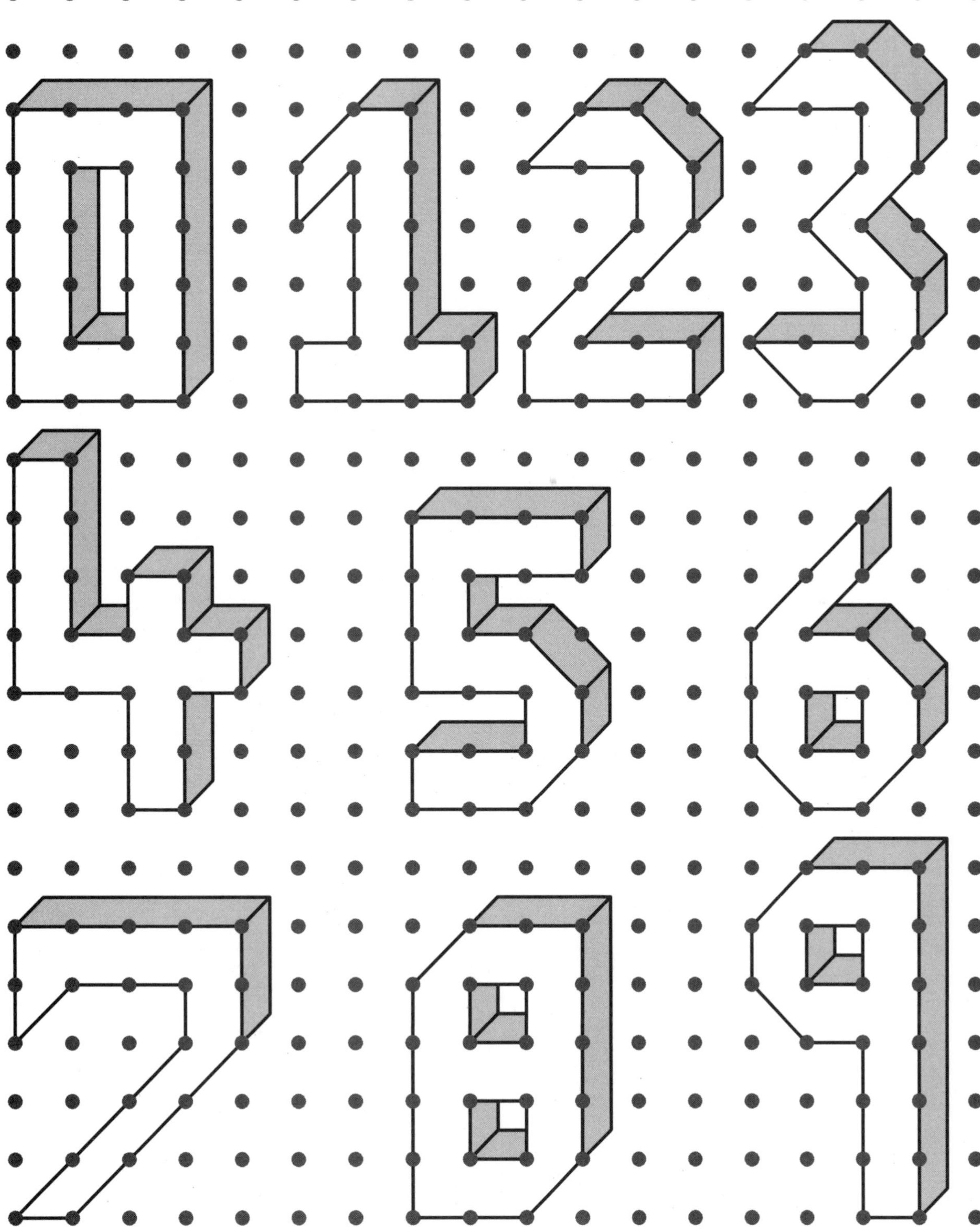

Appendix 2

Recording Solutions (Block Figures 11 and 15, and Block Buildings 3–12)

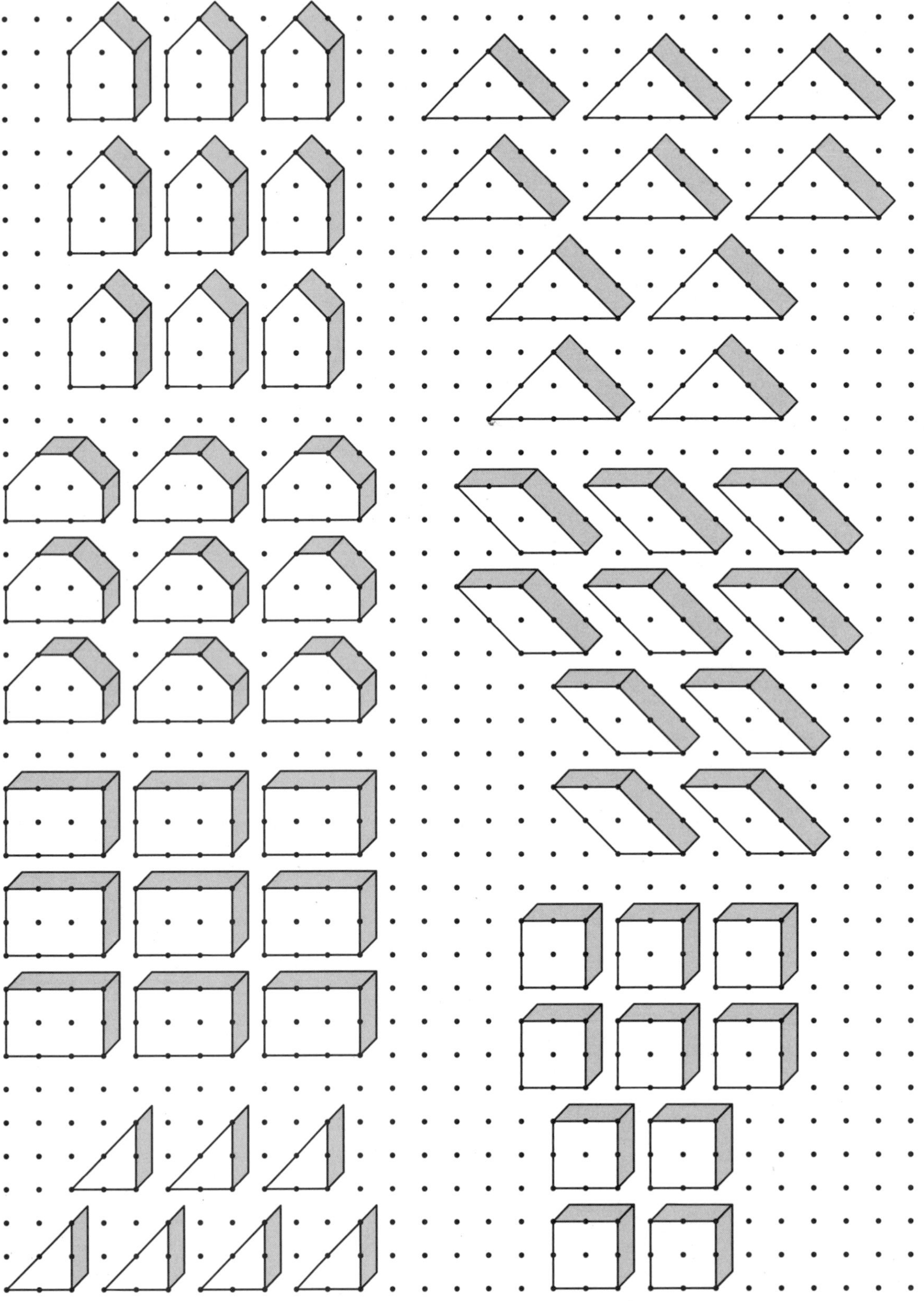

Appendix 3

Recording Solutions (Block Buildings 13–16, and Symmetry Patterns 2–16)

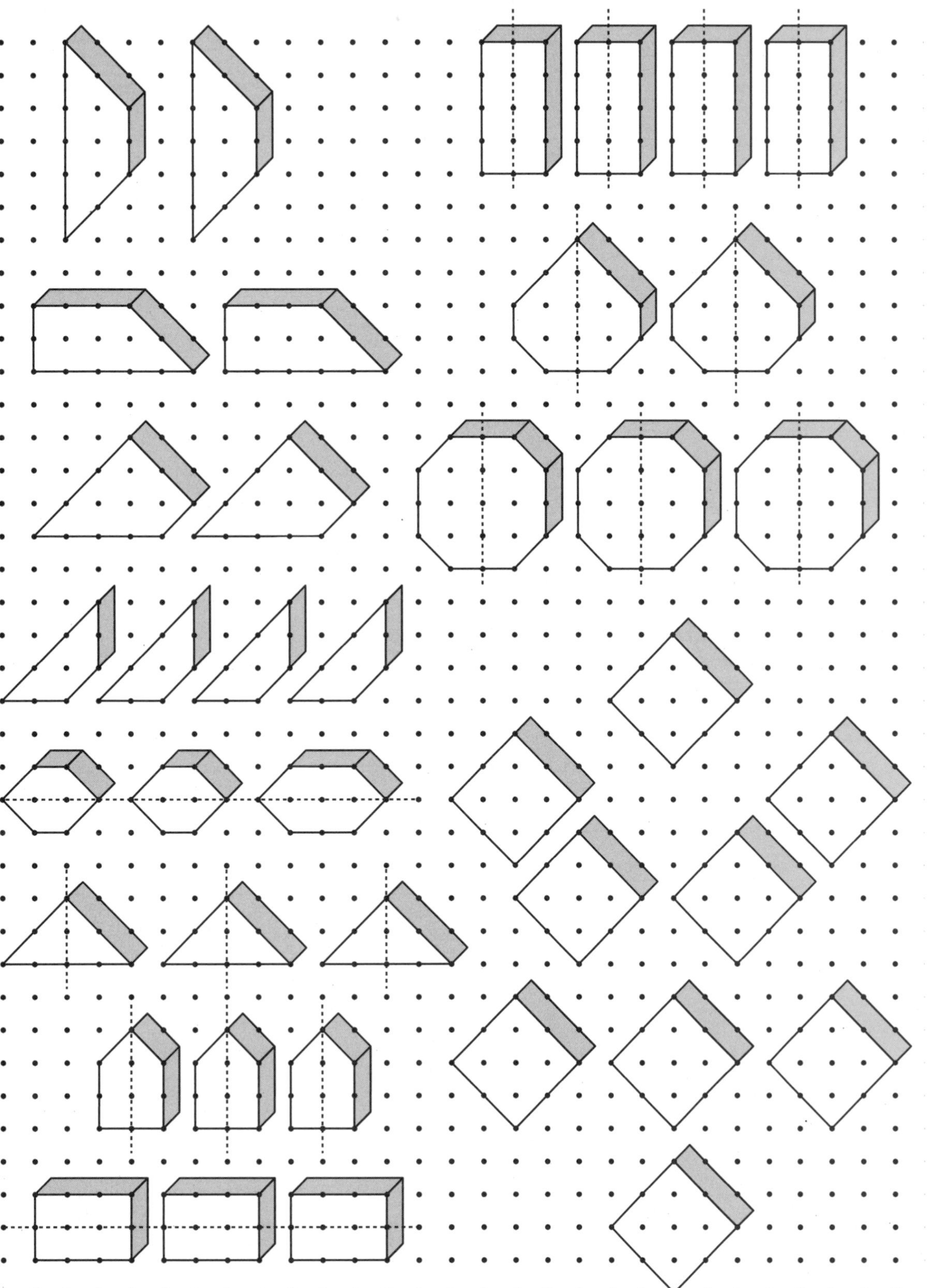

1-Centimeter Dot Paper

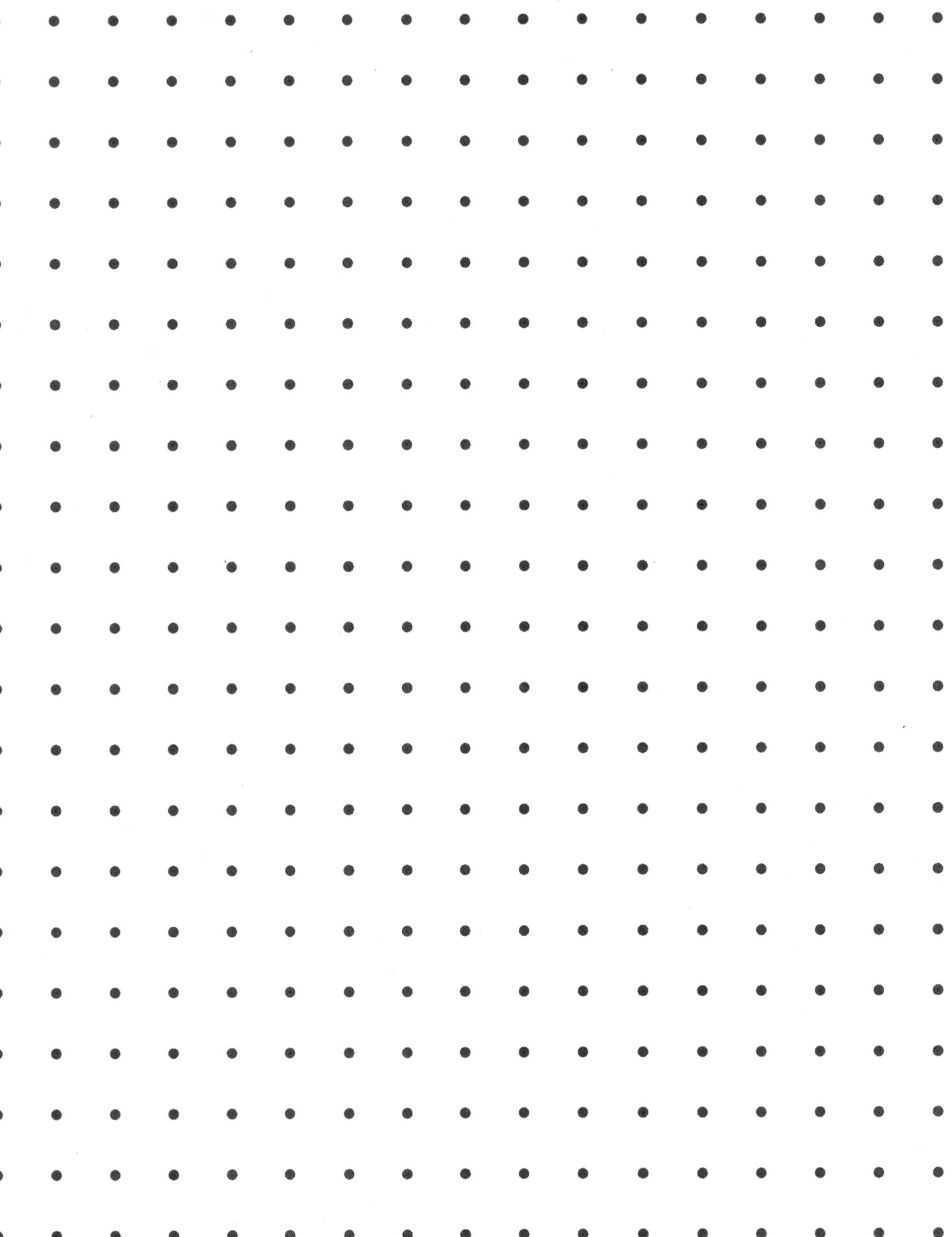

Appendix 5

$\frac{1}{4}$-Inch Dot Paper

Tangram References and Resource Materials

From Cuisenaire Company of America, Inc., White Plains, New York:

- Fair, Jan. *Tangram Treasury*, Book A, 1987.
- *the Super Source®—Tangrams* (K–2), 1996.
- *the Super Source®—Tangrams* (3–4), 1996.
- Sales, Christie and Jeffry. *Tangram Frames*, 1995.

From Creative Publications, Mountain View California:

- Foster, Thomas. *Tangram Patterns*, 1977.
- Seymour, Dale. *Tangramath*, 1971.

From Dale Seymour Publications, White Plains New York:

- Educational Development Center. *ESS Tangram Cards*, set of three, 1988.

From Dover Publications, New York:

- Johnston, Susan. *The Fun with Tangrams Kit*, 1977.
- Johnston, Susan. *Tangrams ABC Kit*, 1979.
- Loyd, Sam. *The Eighth Book of Tan: 700 Tangrams by Sam Loyd*, 1968.
- Read, Ronald. *Tangrams: 330 Puzzles*, 1972.

From Ideal School Supply Company, Alsip, Illinois:

- Goodnow, Judy. *Math Discoveries with Tangrams*, 1994.

From W. H. Freeman, New York:

- Gardner, Martin. *Time Travel and Other Mathematical Bewilderments*, 1988, pp. 27–54.

Answers and Hints

Key: LTP = large triangular prism, MTP = medium triangular prism, STP = small triangular prism, C = cube, P = parallelepiped.

Block Basics 1

Since the purpose is to build as high as possible, any combination that stands is acceptable. It is possible to use all 14 blocks to get a building 13 stories high (two blocks on the first level, one on the remaining levels).

Block Basics 2

Any combination that stands is acceptable. It is difficult, but possible to use all 14 blocks.

Block Basics 3

Using a cube as the base presents a challenge when trying to stack all 14 blocks! Students can stack blocks on the rectangle rather easily if they use the longest side of the LTP as a bottom, as shown below.

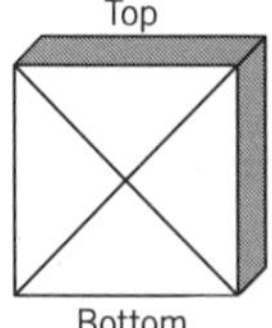

Block Basics 4

Red area: 2 LTPs, 2 STPs, total is 4
Blue area: 2 LTPs, 2 STPs, total is 4
Orange area: 2 Cs, total is 2
Yellow area: 2 MTPs, total is 2
Green area: 2 Ps, total is 2

Block Basics 5

Students place the blocks on the outlines shown.
LTPs in top row: red, blue
MTPs in left middle: yellow
STPs in right middle: red, blue
Ps on left bottom row: green
Cs on right bottom row: orange

Block Basics 6

Place any square face of the cubes on the orange square shapes.
Place any square face of the STPs on the red and blue square shapes.
Place any square face of the Ps on the green square shapes.

Block Basics 7

Place the rectangular faces of the STPs on the blue and red rectangles.
Place either smaller rectangular faces of the MTPs on the yellow rectangles.
Place either rectangular faces of the Ps on the green rectangles.

Block Basics 8

Place the larger rectangular faces of the MTPs on the yellow rectangles.
Place the smaller rectangular faces of the LTPs on the blue and red smaller rectangles.
Place the long rectangular faces of the LTPs on the blue and red larger rectangles.

Block Basics 9

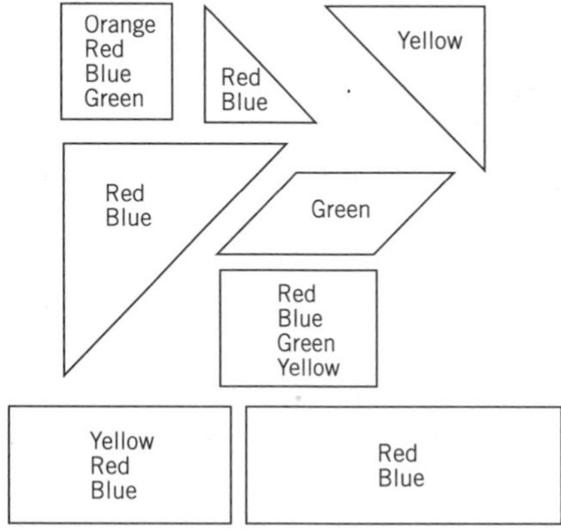

Block Basics 10

Match shapes as shown; no; red and blue; yellow; red and blue; 5

Block Basics 11

Match shapes as shown; 6; 1; 6; 3; 5; 3

Block Basics 12

1. 2 STPs

2. 2 MTPs

Block Basics 13

Note: There are other possible arrangements.

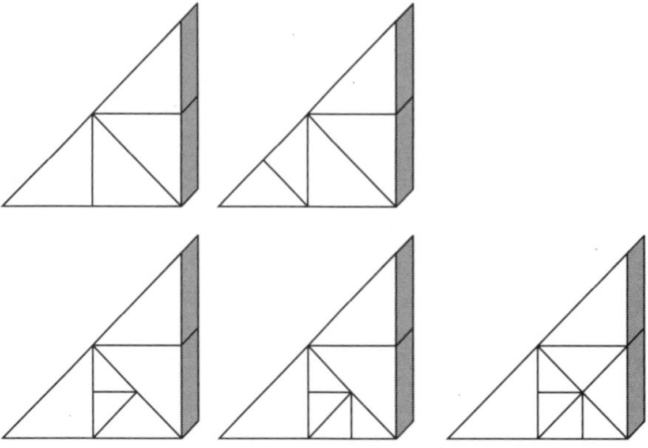

Answers and Hints

Block Basics 14

1. 

2. levels one and two: 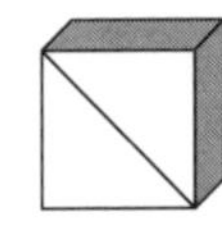

3. 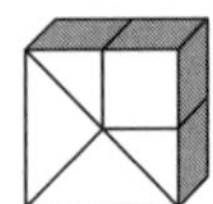 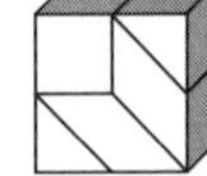

Block Basics 15

1. 

2. 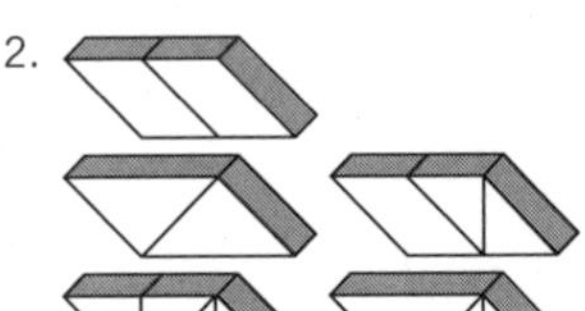

Block Basics 16

Note: There are other possible arrangements.

Challenge:

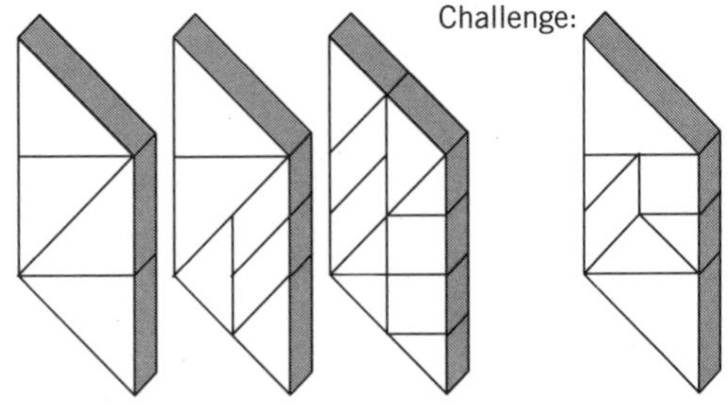

Block Basics 17

Name	Color(s)	Number of Faces	Number of Edges	Number of Vertices
Cube	Orange	6	12	8
Small Triangular Prism	Red or Blue	5	9	6
Medium Triangular Prism	Yellow	5	9	6
Large Triangular Prism	Red or Blue	5	9	6
Parallel-epiped	Green	6	12	8

Block Figures 1

Fill in the outlines as shown.

Block Figures 2

A B C D

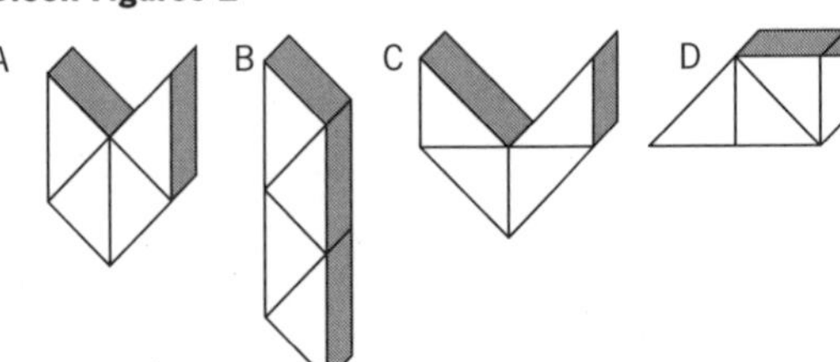

Block Figures 3

A B C

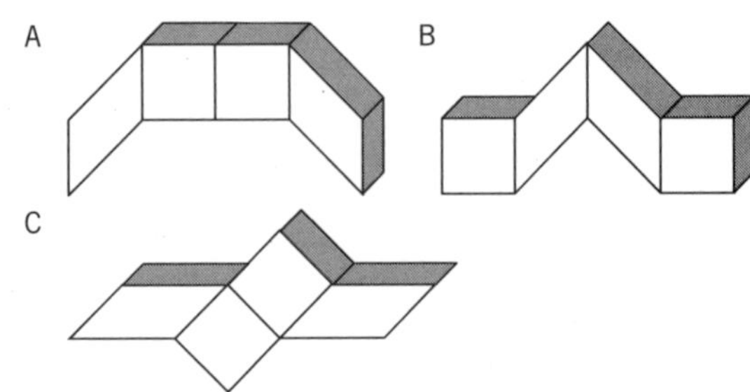

Block Figures 4

A

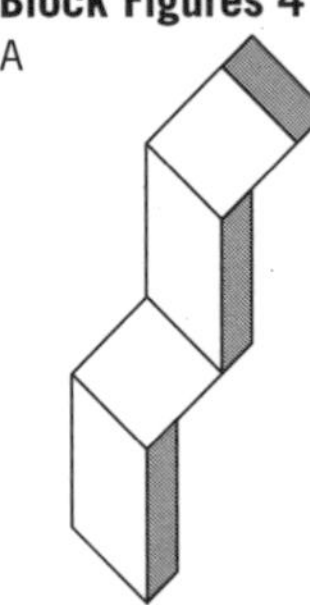

B

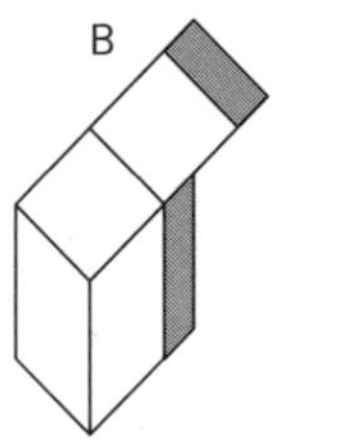

C

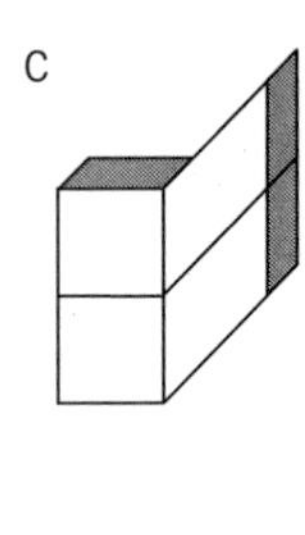

Block Figures 5

1. Fill in the outlines as shown.

Block Figures 6

1. A

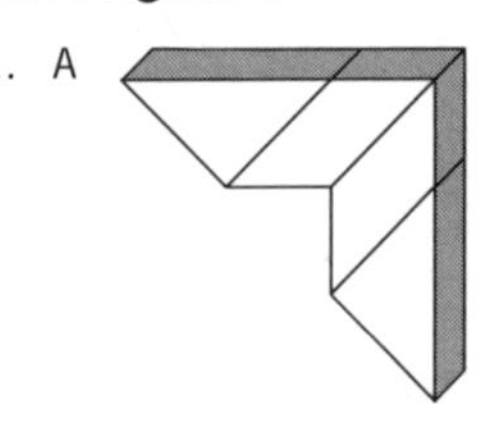

B

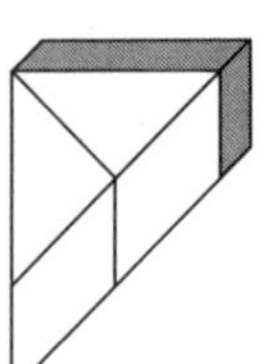

C

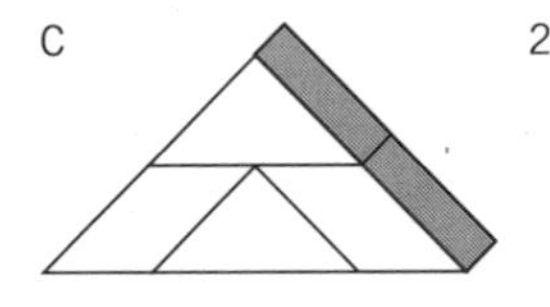

2. D

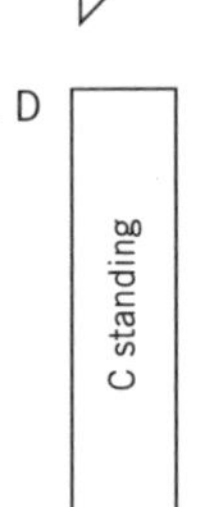

Note: There are other possible arrangements.

Block Figures 7

Fill in the outlines as shown.

Block Figures 8

Note: There are other possible arrangements.

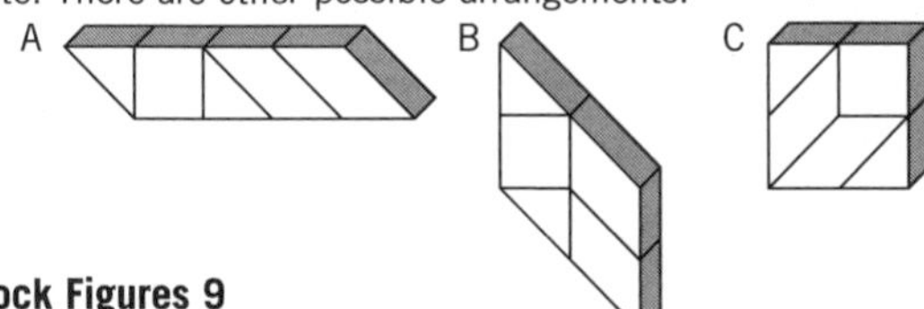

Block Figures 9

These answers assume that the top and bottom surfaces are flat triangles. Some students may fill the outlines so the top surface resembles peaks and valleys.

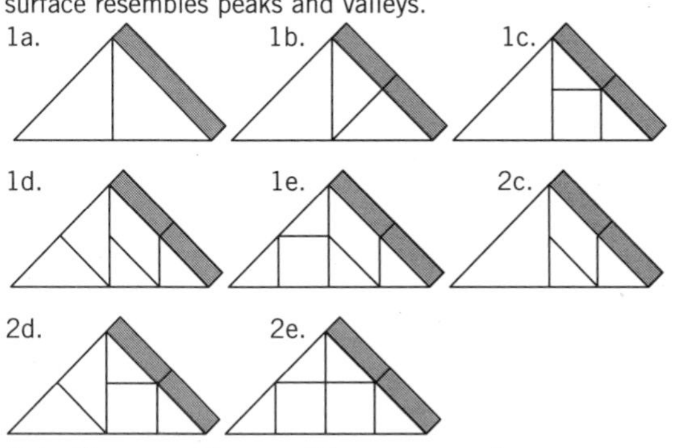

Note: There are other possible arrangements.

Block Figures 10

These answers assume that the top and bottom surfaces are flat pentagons.

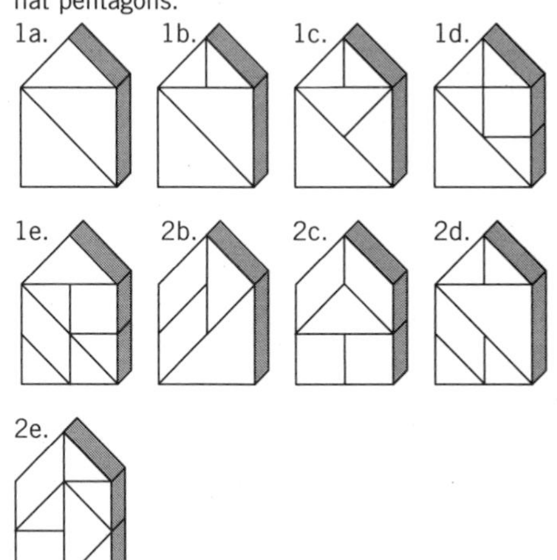

Note: There are other possible arrangements.

Block Figures 11

Answers will vary. Some may be the same as Block Figures 10.

Block Figures 12

These answers assume that the top and bottom surfaces are flat hexagons.

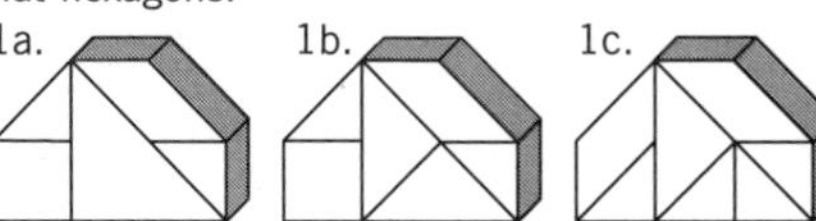

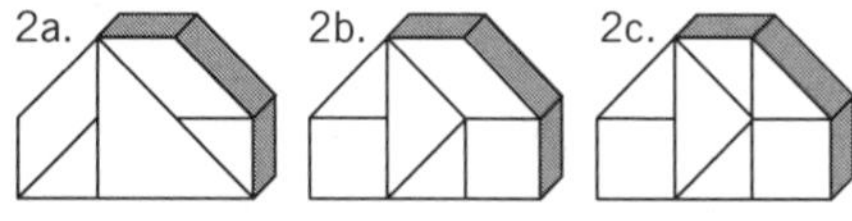

Note: There are other possible arrangements.

Block Figures 13

Answers will vary. Some may be the same as Block Figures 12.

Block Figures 14

These answers assume that the top and bottom surfaces are flat rectangles

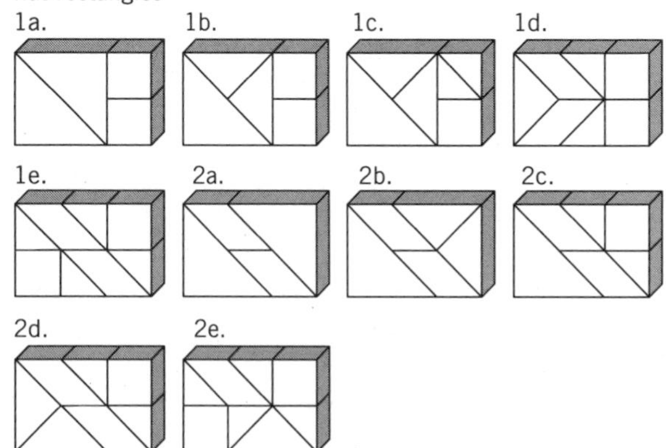

Note: There are other possible arrangements.

Block Figures 15

Answers will vary. Some may be the same as Block Figures 12.

Block Figures 16 through 25

Note: There are other possible arrangements.

Block Buildings 1

1. Stack blocks on their triangular faces.
2. Set STPs on large rectangular faces, triangles touching.
3. Set STPs on square faces, triangles touching.
4. They all have triangular faces touching. They all have the same shape. Other correct answers acceptable.

Block Buildings 2

1. Stack blocks on their triangular faces.
2. Set MTPs on large rectangular faces and STPs on square faces.
3. Set MTPs on small rectangular faces. Set STPs on large rectangular faces and paired with second STP resting against first with square sides touching.
4. They are all stacked the same way, just resting on different sides. Other answers possible.

Block Buildings 3

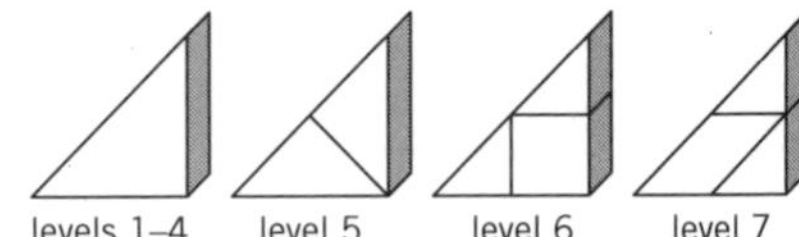

levels 1–4 level 5 level 6 level 7

Note: There are other possible arrangements.

Block Buildings 4

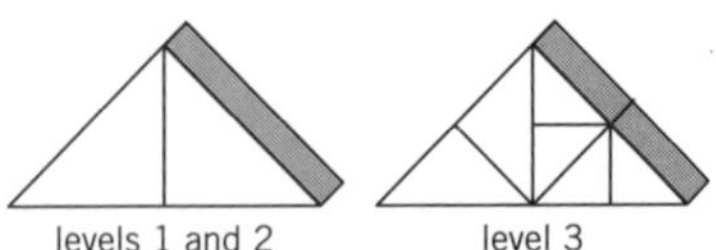

levels 1 and 2 level 3

Note: There are other possible arrangements.

Block Buildings 5

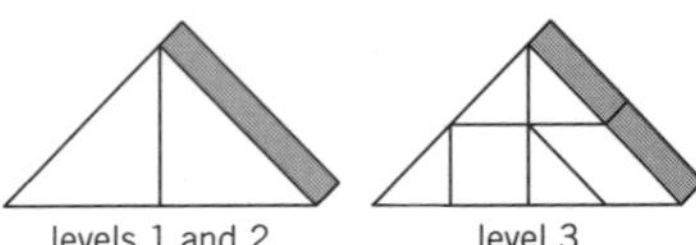

levels 1 and 2 level 3

Note: There are other possible arrangements.

Block Buildings 6

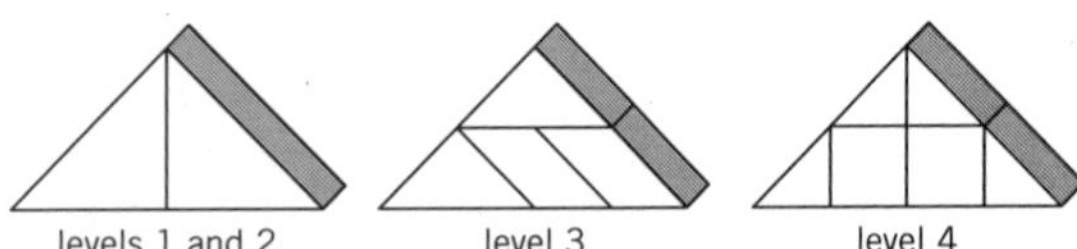

levels 1 and 2 level 3 level 4

Note: There are other possible arrangements.

Block Buildings 7

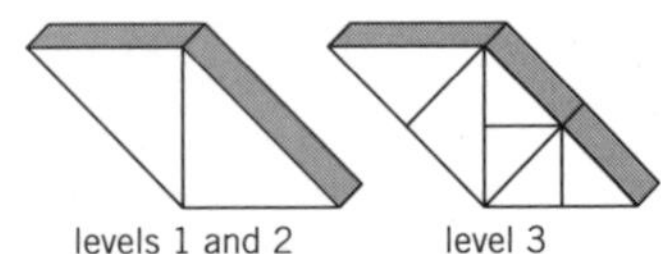

levels 1 and 2 level 3

Note: There are other possible arrangements.

Block Buildings 8

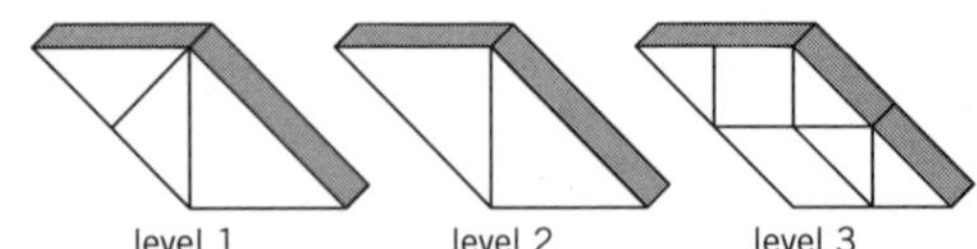

level 1 level 2 level 3

Note: There are other possible arrangements.

Block Buildings 9

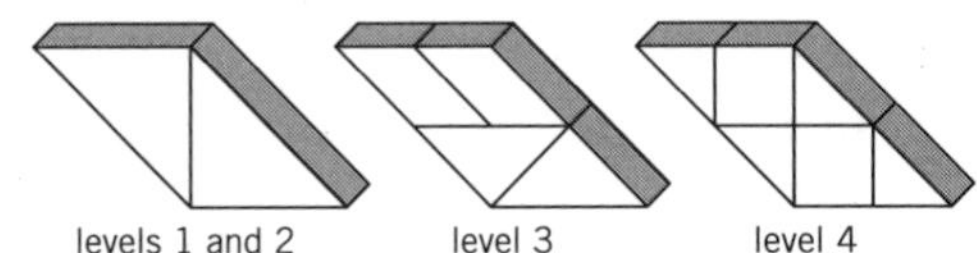

levels 1 and 2 level 3 level 4

Note: There are other possible arrangements.

Block Buildings 10

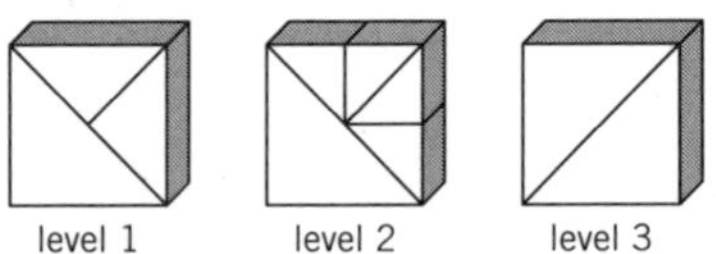

level 1 level 2 level 3

Note: There are other possible arrangements.

Block Buildings 11

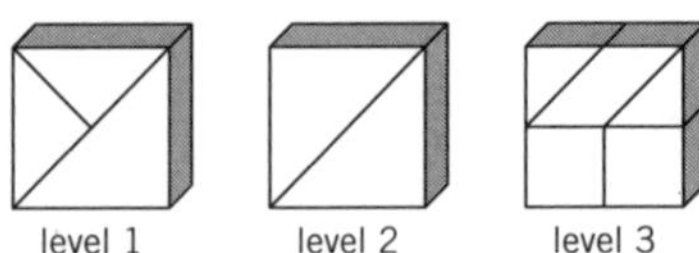

level 1 level 2 level 3

Note: There are other possible arrangements.

Block Buildings 12

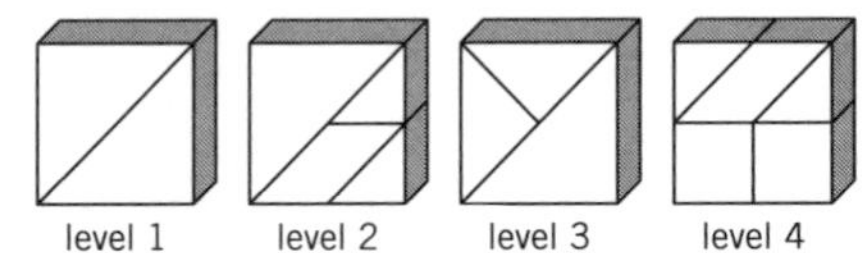

level 1 level 2 level 3 level 4

Note: There are other possible arrangements.

Block Buildings 13

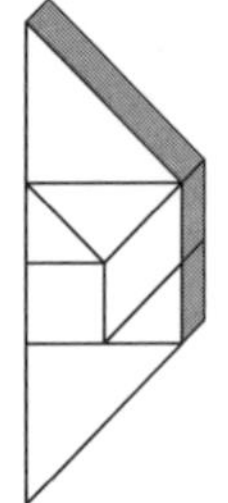

levels 1 and 2

Note: There are other possible arrangements.

Block Buildings 14

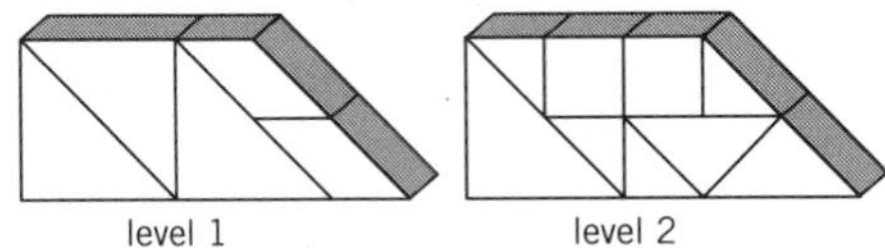

Note: There are other possible arrangements.

Block Buildings 15

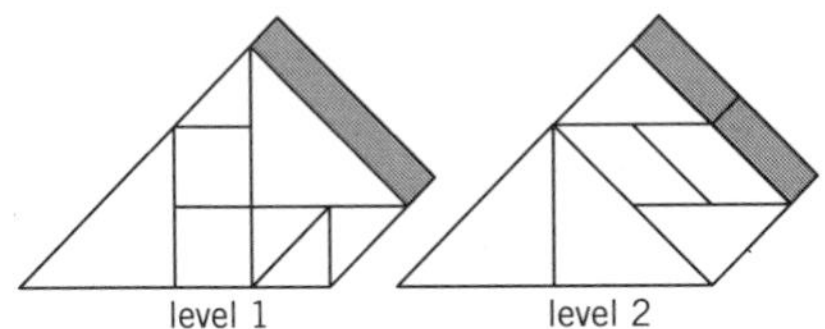

Note: There are other possible arrangements.

Block Buildings 16

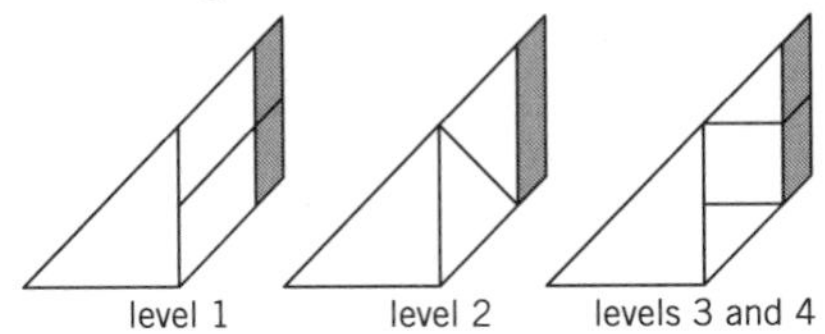

Note: There are other possible arrangements.

Symmetry Patterns 1

Fill in outlines as shown.

Symmetry Patterns 2

3.

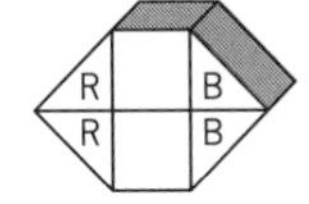

Symmetry Patterns 3

3.

Symmetry Patterns 4

3.

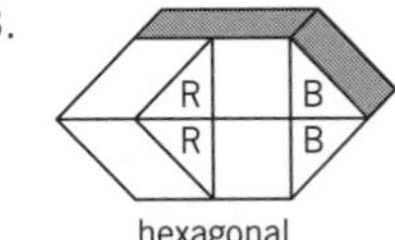

Symmetry Patterns 5

1a. Use two same-color LTPs.
1b. through 1d., see below.
2.

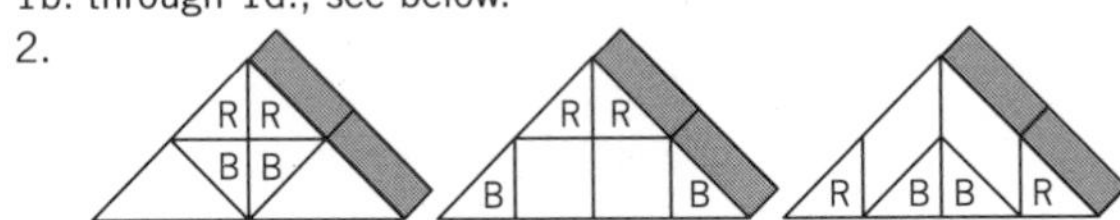

Note: There are other possible arrangements.

Symmetry Patterns 6

1a. 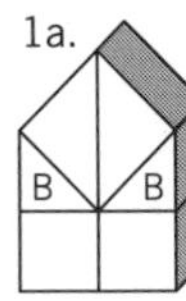 1b. 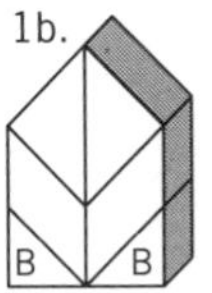 1c. 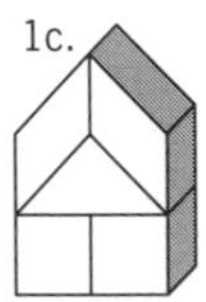

2. See above. Note: There are other possible arrangements.

Symmetry Patterns 7

1a. 1b. 1c.

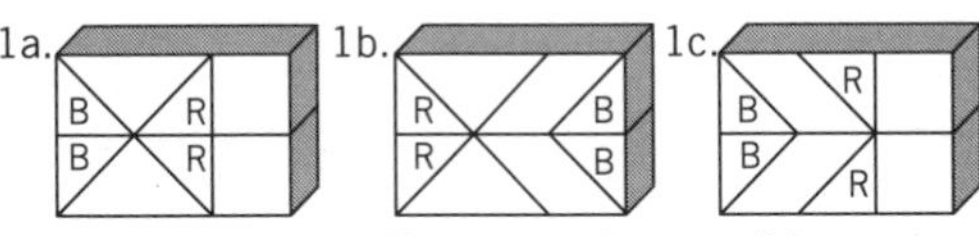

2. See above. Note: There are other possible arrangements.

Symmetry Patterns 8

1.

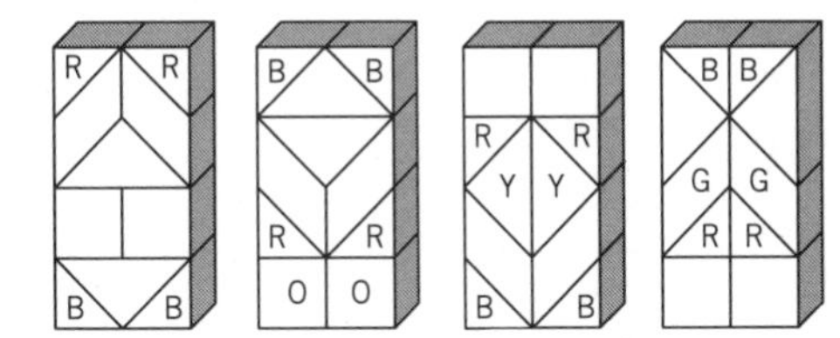

2. See above. Note: There are other possible arrangements.

Symmetry Patterns 9

1.

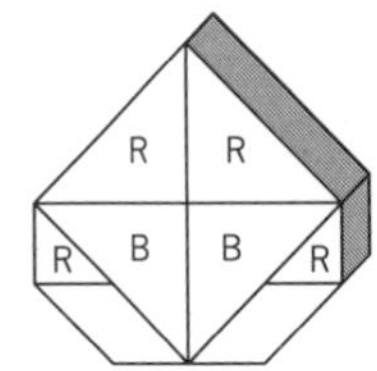

2. See above. Note: There are other possible arrangements.

Symmetry Patterns 10

1a. 1b. 1c.

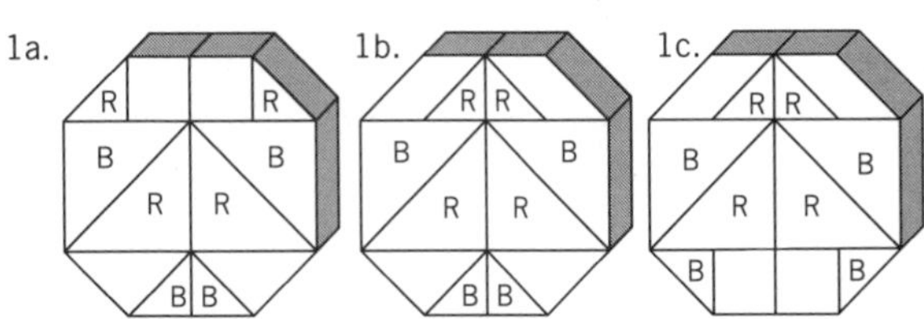

2. See above. Note: There are other possible arrangements.

Symmetry Patterns 11

1.

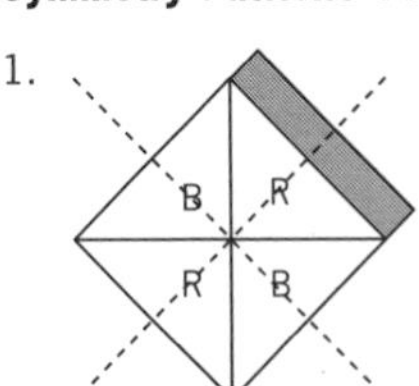

2. 2
3. See above.

Answers and Hints

Symmetry Patterns 12

1.

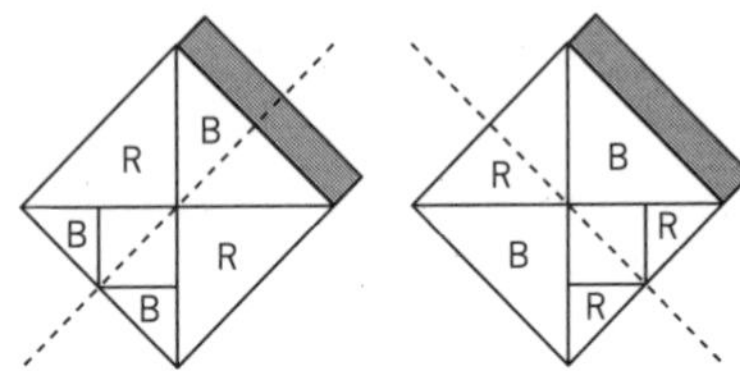

2. See above.

Symmetry Patterns 13

1.

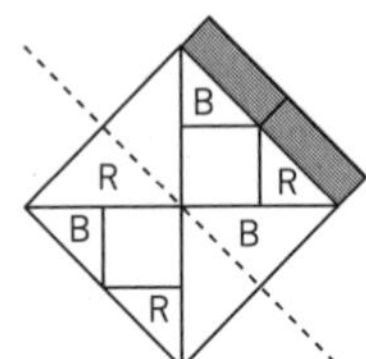

2. See above.

Symmetry Patterns 14

1.

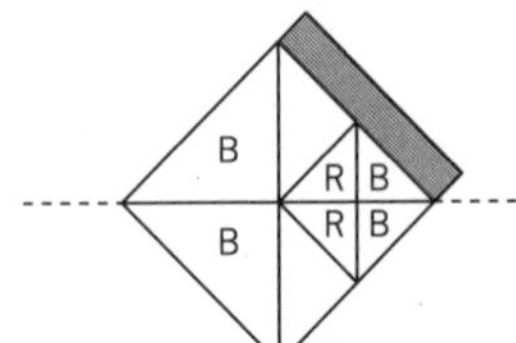

2. See above.

Symmetry Patterns 15

1a. 1b.

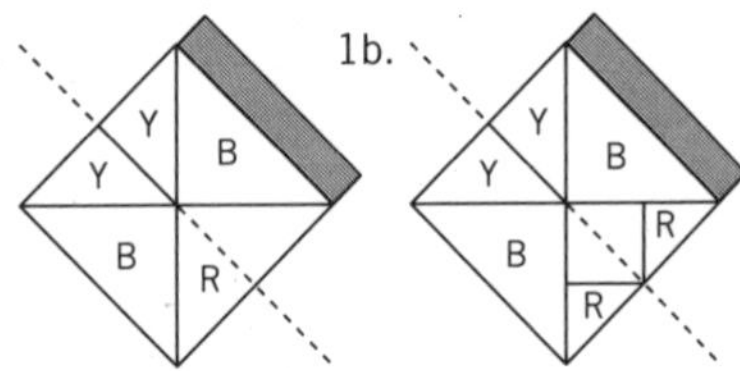

1c.

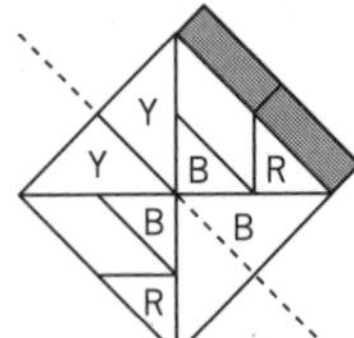

Other solutions may be found with no line of symmetry.

2. See above. Note: There are other possible arrangements.

Symmetry Patterns 16

1.

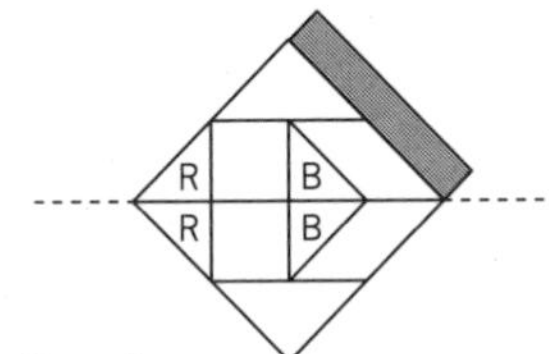

2. See above.

Puzzles and Designs 1

Arrange blocks as shown.

Puzzles and Designs 2

Arrange blocks as shown.

Puzzles and Designs 3

Arrange blocks as shown.

Puzzles and Designs 4

Arrange blocks as shown.

Puzzles and Designs 5

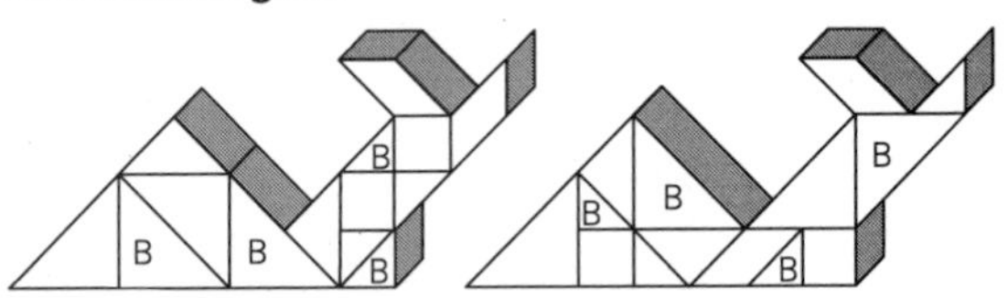

Note: There are other possible arrangements.

Puzzles and Designs 6

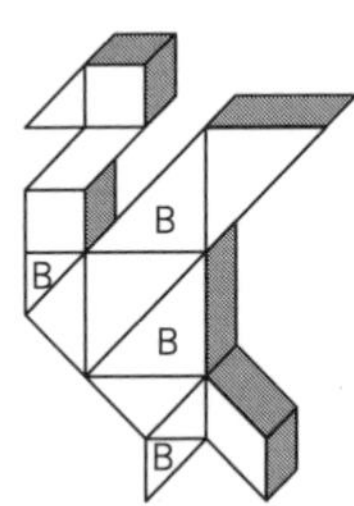

Note: There are other possible arrangements.

Puzzles and Designs 7

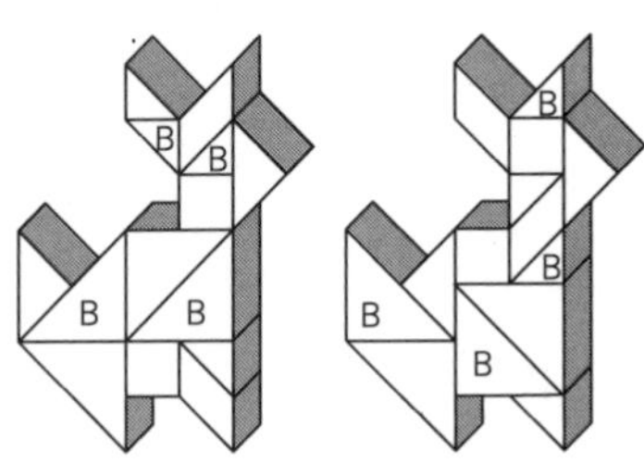

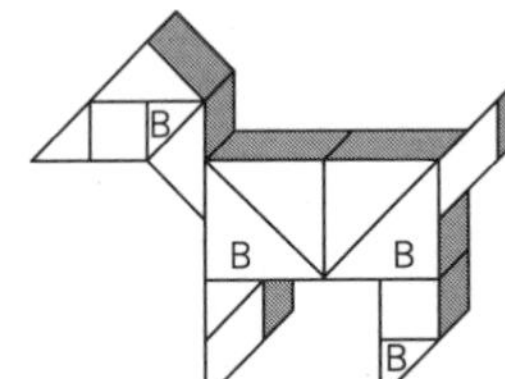

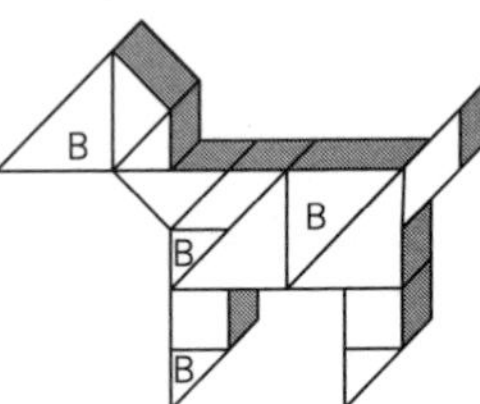

Note: There are other possible arrangements.

Puzzles and Designs 8

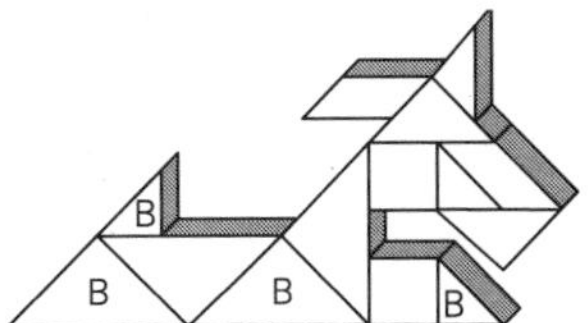

Puzzles and Designs 9

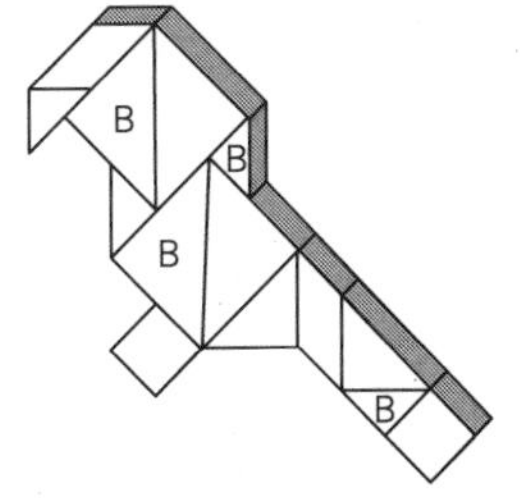

Puzzles and Designs 10

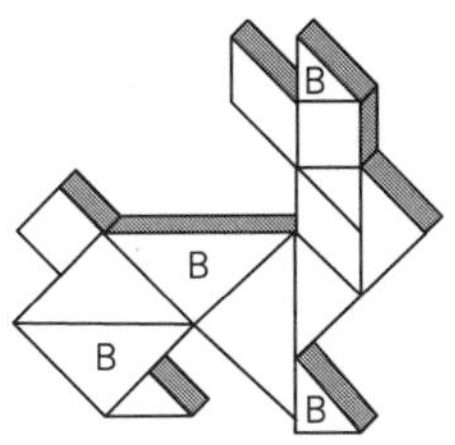

Puzzles and Designs 11

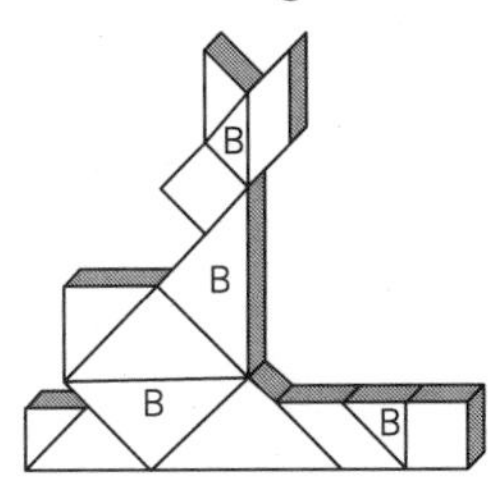

Puzzles and Designs 12

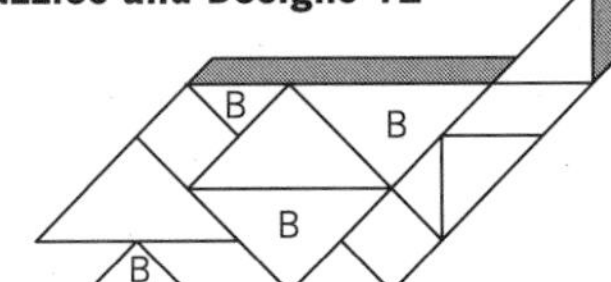

Puzzles and Designs 13

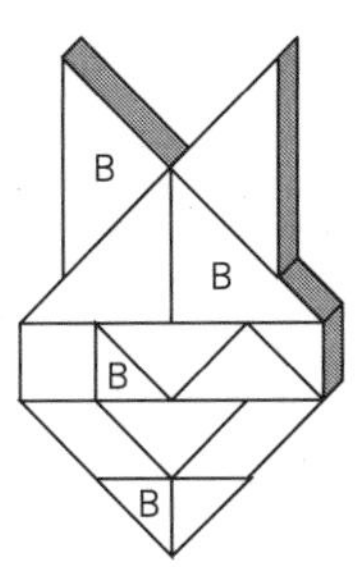

Puzzles and Designs 14

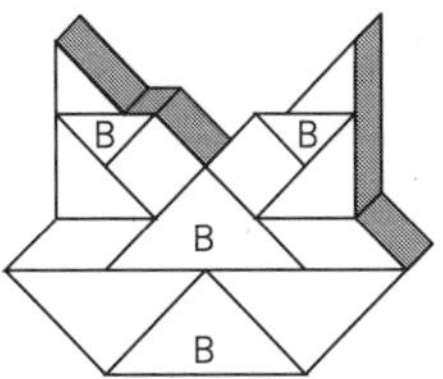

Puzzles and Designs 15

Blocks	Vertical Sides
1	3
2	3
3	5
4	6
5	6
6	6
7	7
8	8
9	7
10	6
11	9
12	12
13	13
14	14

There are four arrangements with six sides. The number of sides goes up and down. At the end the number of blocks is the same as the number of sides.

Puzzles and Designs 16

Blocks	Vertical Sides
1	3
2	4
3	6
4	8
5	8
6	8
7	10
8	12
9	14
10	16
11	17
12	18
13	19
14	20

The number of sides stays the same or gets greater. There are three arrangements with eight sides.

Patterns and Designs 17

Blocks	Vertical Sides
1	3
2	4
3	5
4	6
5	7
6	8
7	9
8	10
9	11
10	12
11	13
12	14
13	16
14	18

The number of sides goes up one each time except for the last two arrangements.

Puzzles and Designs 18

Blocks	Vertical Sides
1	4
2	8
3	7
4	6
5	7
6	8
7	8
8	8
9	10
10	12
11	13
12	14
13	14
14	14

The number of sides goes up and down. The last three blocks do not add more sides.

Puzzles and Designs 19

Blocks	Vertical Sides
1	3
2	4
3	4
4	4
5	6
6	8
7	9
8	10
9	10
10	10
11	9
12	8
13	8
14	8

There are three arrangements with four and ten sides and four arrangements with eight sides. The number of sides goes up, then down.

Puzzles and Designs 20

Blocks	Vertical Sides
1	4
2	6
3	7
4	10
5	11
6	12
7	11
8	10
9	11
10	9
11	10
12	11
13	11
14	11

There are three arrangements of ten sides followed by eleven sides. There are six arrangements of eleven sides.

Puzzles and Designs 21

Blocks	Vertical Sides
1	4
2	4
3	4
4	4
5	6
6	8
7	10
8	12
9	12
10	12
11	14
12	16
13	18
14	20

There are only even numbers. The number of sides always goes up.